Decoding the
Japanese Mind
through Expressions

Rokuro Morita

Translators
Mari and Daniel M. Williams

Supervising Editor
Kiyotada Tazaki

ASK Publishing Co., Ltd.

Foreword

It has been my pleasure to be associated with Mr. Rokuro Morita, author of the original Japanese edition, *Understanding the Japanese Mind through Language and Culture*.

Graduated from Waseda University, one of the most prestigious private universities in Japan with a major in East Asian philosophy, Mr. Morita showed special interest in the historical and cultural linguistic transmission from China to Japan. Although Japanese language was greatly influenced by Chinese, there remain substantial differences between the two. When he started teaching Japanese language and culture in Beijing, at the University of International Business and Economics, he further explored the cultural differences between Japan and China. His efforts later crystalized in the form of his original book. Books like Daisetsu Suzuki's *Zen Buddhism and Its Influence on Japanese Culture* (1938) and Ruth Benedict's *The Chrysanthemum and the Sword* (1946) have served as introductory references to Japanese culture. However, I believe this book by Mr. Morita is the first venture to organize the unique aspects of Japanese culture by common expressions, explained in detail from historical background to current motivations. We are indeed fortunate that ASK Publishing has the vision to support this project, and to keep the work up-to-date. Established in 2008, and specializing in language and culture textbooks, such as English, Japanese, Chinese, Korean, and Vietnamese, ASK is a highly active and influential publishing company.

The original book was geared mainly for Japanese readers or Japanese learners who are interested in understanding characteristics of the Japanese culture. For this book to be translated into English, we had to make numerous adjustments, because the prospective readers are not of the same background. In this regard, I am pleased that we have found an ideal team, an American husband and a Japanese wife, as translators. Daniel M. Williams, a jazz composer and contributor of numerous cultural articles in English to Japanese magazines and periodicals, used to teach English in language schools in Japan. Mari Williams, as senior lecturer in Japanese and French at the University of Miami, is in the strategic position of navigating the linguistic and cultural differences between Japanese and English. Furthermore, the two translators were able to discuss the cross-cultural issues readily at home and work out the best representation of the original book for English speakers.

I hope that this book provides to western readers an absorbing read, a relevant textbook, and a solid reference book.

Supervising Editor Kiyotada Tazaki

Preface

The Japanese archipelago is sequestered by the sea. We do not have a history of being dominated by outside powers, as China was, and we do not have a melting pot culture of disparate peoples, as they do in the United States. Moreover, due to a policy of self-isolation, Japanese people had little opportunity to interact with outsiders for long periods of time before the modern era. This may explain why non-Japanese people find the mysteries of our language and culture so hard to grasp.

In this book, I identify characteristic words and expressions that Japanese people commonly use in daily life and elaborate on the background behind our peculiar sensitivities and ideas. In addition, I explain many of the life values that we have long held beautiful and dear, such as *bushidou* (the way of the warrior) and *wabi-sabi* (an aesthetic sense in Japanese art).

If you wish to understand the true meanings that underlie the Japanese language or to know how and why Japanese people feel a certain way in certain situations, I believe this book will be resourceful. I hope you can better understand why Japanese people bow, refrain from doing some things, laugh or get angry, and the kind of language we use for those and many other situations.

My friend, Mari Williams, translated this book in collaboration of her husband, Daniel M. Williams. With Mari's knowledge of the Japanese language as a language teacher and writer, and Daniel's input as an English speaker, writer, editor, and former resident in Japan, I believe they succeeded in presenting the delicacies of the Japanese language in natural English.

I am deeply honored and grateful to Professor Kiyotada Tazaki, who is an eminent Japanese authority in TEFL (Teaching English as a Foreign Language) and Area Studies in the U.S.A. for his substantial involvement and invaluable advice as supervising editor.

Finally, I would like to express my sincerest gratitude to Mr. Osami Amaya, president of ASK Publishing Company, who has lent his unwavering support from the beginning for all editions of this book, and also to Ms. Kaho Matsuo, who, as editor, managed every detail of the look and feel of the book.

Author Rokuro Morita

Translators' Notes

As a Japanese teacher, Mari often tells her students, "Japanese people can read your mind, so if you want to live in Japan, watch out!" As an American who lived in Japan for several years, Dan told Mari that people often seemed to read his thoughts and reacted before he knew them himself. We knew there was something going on in Japan, but we could not explain it. After reading and translating this book, we were finally able to decode these and many other mysteries of the Japanese mind.

In this book, Mr. Morita has managed to identify and label the salient aspects of Japanese society that can mystify foreigners. He offers lively examples of the target Japanese phrases in context, leaving the reader with a treasure trove of useful expressions surrounding each topic. He also explains them from historical and cultural perspectives with scholarly references, which can serve as jumping-off points for further reading.

No language can be transformed perfectly into another because every language has its own history and culture behind it. However, especially with Japanese, it is sometimes nearly impossible to convey the assumed knowledge that underlies the language into a natural form in English. Therefore, in this book, we present the Japanese conversations at the following levels.

- First, the language is presented in native Japanese script, using *kanji* (Chinese characters) with *furigana* above each character to indicate the reading, and *hiragana* and *katakana* (the two forms of Japanese phonetic syllabary). The terms in bold follow Mr. Morita's key talking points.
- Second, the reading is presented as *romaji* (the phonetic reading in the Roman alphabet). *Romaji* in bold follows the bolded Japanese script.
- Finally, the English translation is at the bottom, which may diverge from the literal translation and word order to convey the feeling and intent of the Japanese.

高校生になったら、勉強もスポーツも**がんばります**。
Koukousei ni nattara, benkyou mo supootsu mo **ganbari masu**.
When I begin high school, I will work hard at my studies and in sports.

When we present target words or expressions, we sometimes give the literal translation, followed by the true meaning, if required to convey the concept. The difference between the two should be obvious.

根回し (***nemawashi***, digging round root, behind-the-scenes negotiation)

We hope these layers of translation will interest readers and should assist Japanese language learners and those who wish to delve into the Japanese language.

Dan and Mari Williams

Notes Concerning Romanization

To balance sound and function, the Japanese in the book is Romanized mostly using the Traditional Hepburn system of *romaji*, which is similar to the text we enter into a Japanese word processor, with some exceptions.

1. Integrated diacritical marks are not used, as in the Modified Hepburn system.

    Example: お母さん (mother)　　*okaasan*　　instead of *okāsan*

2. The sound indicated by the *hiragana* ん is written with "n" regardless of what sound follows it.

    Example: がんばる (to endeavor)　　*ganbaru*　　instead of *gambaru*

3. Because the *hiragana* ん changes its pronunciation when followed by vowel sounds, an apostrophe is employed after the "n."

    Example: 繁栄 (prosperity)　　*han'ei*　　instead of *hanei*

4. Whereas Japanese text does not use spaces, spaces are added between words in *romaji* to differentiate meanings and functions.

    Example: 内と外 (inside and outside)　　*uchi to soto*　　instead of *uchitosoto*

5. *Hiragana* particles appear as separate words. To represent their spoken sound, は is spelled "*wa*" instead of "*ha*," へ is spelled "*e*" instead of "*he*," and を is spelled "*o*" instead of "*wo*."

    Example: 父は本を読む。(Father reads a book.)
    Chichi wa hon o yomu.　　instead of *Chichi ha hon wo yomu.*

6. Japanese words that appear in standard English, people and place names, and titles of known literary works retain their traditional spelling and are not italicized.

    Example: 東京　　Tokyo　　instead of *toukyou*

Contents

Foreword iii

Preface iv

Translators' Notes v

Notes Concerning Romanization vi

Chapter 1 内と外を分ける
Uchi to Soto o Wakeru, To Distinguish Inside from Outside

- 1-1 内と外 *Uchi to Soto*, Inside and Outside ⋯⋯⋯⋯⋯⋯⋯ 2
- 1-2 世間 *Seken*, Society/the world ⋯⋯⋯⋯⋯⋯⋯⋯⋯⋯⋯ 8
- 1-3 しつけ *Shitsuke*, Discipline ⋯⋯⋯⋯⋯⋯⋯⋯⋯⋯⋯⋯ 12
- 1-4 けじめ *Kejime*, Distinction ⋯⋯⋯⋯⋯⋯⋯⋯⋯⋯⋯⋯ 16
- 1-5 素直 *Sunao*, Obedience and Innocence ⋯⋯⋯⋯⋯⋯⋯ 19
- 1-6 甘える *Amaeru*, To Rely on Another's Love or Kindness ⋯ 21

❀ Everyday Conversations 1: Greeting, Farewell, and Gratitude ⋯⋯ 24

Chapter 2 他人の目を意識する
Tanin no Me o Ishiki Suru, To Be Mindful of the Public Eye

- 2-1 人目 *Hitome*, Public Eye/Perception by Others ⋯⋯⋯ 28
- 2-2 恥 *Haji*, Shame ⋯⋯⋯⋯⋯⋯⋯⋯⋯⋯⋯⋯⋯⋯⋯⋯ 32
- 2-3 照れる *Tereru*, To Be Abashed ⋯⋯⋯⋯⋯⋯⋯⋯⋯⋯ 36

Chapter 3 周囲に配慮する
Shuui ni Hairyo Suru, To Consider the People around Us

- 3-1 遠慮 *Enryo*, Restraint ⋯⋯⋯⋯⋯⋯⋯⋯⋯⋯⋯⋯⋯⋯ 40
- 3-2 気をつかう *Ki o Tsukau*, To Be Concerned ⋯⋯⋯⋯⋯ 45
- 3-3 人並み *Hitonami*, Average or Like Others ⋯⋯⋯⋯⋯ 49
- 3-4 空気を読む *Kuuki o Yomu*, To Read the Situation ⋯⋯ 52

❀ Everyday Conversations 2: The Real Intentions ⋯⋯⋯⋯⋯⋯⋯ 56

Chapter 4 人間関係を大切にする
Ningen Kankei o Taisetsu ni Suru, To Value Relationships

- 4-1 つきあい *Tsukiai*, Obligatory Companionship ⋯⋯⋯⋯ 60

4-2	愛想	*Aiso*, Amiability	63
4-3	礼儀	*Reigi*, Manners and Etiquette	66
4-4	本音と建前	*Honne to Tatemae*, True Feelings and Official Stance	70
4-5	おかげさま	*Okagesama*, Your Benevolence	73

❀ Everyday Conversations 3: Showing Agreement or Comprehension ········ 76

Chapter 5 表現を抑える
Hyougen o Osaeru, To Restrain Personal Expressions

5-1	控えめ	*Hikaeme*, Restrained or Moderate	80
5-2	ほのめかす	*Honomekasu*, To Give a Hint or Imply	84
5-3	角を立てない	*Kado o Tatenai*, Avoid Offence	89

❀ Everyday Conversations 4: Softening the Impact ········ 92

Chapter 6 精神主義を好む
Seishinshugi o Konomu, To Embrace Spiritualism

6-1	がんばる	*Ganbaru*, To Endeavor	96
6-2	根性	*Konjou*, Willpower	100
6-3	無理	*Muri*, Unreasonable	103
6-4	修行	*Shugyou*, Training, Ascetic Practices	106
6-5	武士道	*Bushidou*, The Way of the Warrior	110

Chapter 7 日本人の価値観
Nihonjin no Kachikan, Japanese Values

7-1	品	*Hin*, Class	116
7-2	やまとなでしこ	*Yamato Nadeshiko*, The Japanese Ideal Woman	119
7-3	派手・地味	*Hade and Jimi*, Flashy and Plain	121
7-4	恩・義理	*On and Giri*, Debt of Gratitude and Sense of Obligation	126
7-5	いさぎよい	*Isagiyoi*, Gallant, Sportsmanlike	130
7-6	もったいない	*Mottainai*, Wasteful	133

❀ Everyday Conversations 5: Apology First and Foremost ········ 137

Selected Bibliography 139

Index 140

About the Author, the Supervising Editor, and the Translators 150

Chapter 1

内と外を分ける

Uchi to Soto o Wakeru

To Distinguish Inside from Outside

内と外 *Uchi to Soto*, Inside and Outside

The perception of 内と外 (*uchi to soto*, inside and outside) is critical in Japanese society. It primarily refers to the dichotomy between one's family and the outside world. The Chinese character 家 (*ie*, house) is also read (***uchi***), and holds the same meaning as 内.

In Japan, the distinction between *uchi* and *soto* begins when we are young, the initial *uchi* being one's home. As we grow older, the border between *uchi* and *soto* shifts, depending on the circumstances. When we consider our school or our company, we say, うちの学校 (*uchi no gakkou*, my school in relation to other schools) and うちの会社 (*uchi no kaisha*, my company in relation to other companies). Likewise, we call outside people and outside groups *soto*. Because of the implied exclusiveness of *uchi*, *soto* is also referred to as よそ (*yoso*, another world).

In childhood, we often envy our friends' families. We become jealous of a friend's new toy, and then plead with our parents to buy us the same thing. For this situation, Japanese parents might make use of the set phrase shown in Example 1.

Example 1

子ども　お母さん、あのおもちゃ買ってよ。みんな持ってるんだよ。

Kodomo　*Okaasan, ano omocha katte yo. Minna motterun da yo.*

Child　Mom, buy me that toy. All the other kids have it.

母親　よそはよそ、うちはうち！がまんしなさい！
Hahaoya **Yoso** wa **yoso**, **uchi** wa **uchi**! Gaman shi nasai!
Mother Their house, their rules. Our house, our rules. Get over it!

Example 2

先生、こんにちは。**うち**の子どもがいつもお世話になっています。
Sensei, konnichiwa. **Uchi** *no kodomo ga itsumo osewa ni natte i masu.*
Hello, Teacher. Thank you for always looking after our child.

Even as adults, our family is still *uchi,* but the distinction between *uchi* and *soto/yoso* can hold broader connotations. For example, we consider our company colleagues *uchi*: うちの会社の人 (*uchi no kaisha no hito*), while people outside of the company are *yoso*. Also, within the company, people in our department are *uchi*: うちの部の人 (*uchi no bu no hito*) and people of the other departments are *yoso*. Even within the same department, people of our project team are *uchi*: うちのチームの人 (*uchi no chiimu no hito*) while people of the other project teams are *yoso*.

Example 3

うちの会社は**よそ**の会社と比べて給料がいい。
Uchi no kaisha wa **yoso** no kaisha to kurabete kyuuryou ga ii.
Compared to the salaries of other companies, ours is better.

Example 4

そっちの部はいいなあ。**うち**の部は残業ばかりだよ。
Socchi no bu wa ii naa. **Uchi** *no bu wa zangyou bakari da yo.*
Your department is good. Ours always makes us work overtime.

3

The distinction between *uchi* and *soto* also needs to be protected. For instance, when a snafu occurs in an organization, and 身内 (*miuchi*, the inner circle) takes care of it without outside help, we call that うちうちで片づける (***uchiuchi de katazukeru***, to clean it up within the group). It means that we will keep the problem inside to prevent it from leaking out to *soto*.

In other examples, we refer to fancy clothes that are not worn in a casual setting as よそ行きの服 (***yosoyuki no fuku***, clothes for the outside world), and we say よそよそしい (***yosoyososhii***, attitude to someone from the outside world) when someone acts in a distant way with an acquaintance, even though they know each other well.

Example 5

もう長いつきあいなんだから、いつまでもそんなに**よそよそしい**話し方をしないで、もっとくだけた話し方をしてよ。

*Mou nagai tsukiai nan da kara, itsumademo sonna ni **yosoyososhii** hanashikata o shinai de, motto kudaketa hanashikata o shite yo.*

Since we've known each other for some time now, don't talk like a stranger; speak freely.

敬語 (*keigo*, honorific language) is used when we talk to superiors or someone we do not know well, for the sake of politeness. However, the use of *keigo* can be interpreted as よそ行き (*yosoyuki*, going outside). Therefore, if we keep using honorific words, our attitude might seem unfriendly to the listener. On the other hand, if the relationship to a person is not close, the nonuse of *keigo* is called speaking なれなれしい (***narenareshii***, too friendly), and the speaker could be shunned.

For Japanese people, the concepts of 内と外 (*uchi to soto*) are vital principles to determine proper speech, attitude, and actions. This perception of always belonging to some group is usually instinctive and natural. However, a predicament occurs when a woman gets married. The distinction between *uchi* and *soto* drastically changes, because she has literally become a member of her husband's family. For her, the *uchi* of her childhood has now become *soto*, and her mother-in-law commonly takes on the role of re-educating her to favor her new family or to protect its reputation.

Example 6
あなたはもう**うち**の人なんだから、ちゃんとして下さいよ。
*Anata wa mou **uchi** no hito nan da kara, chanto shite kudasai yo.*
You are now part of this family. Please act accordingly.

As you have seen, the lines between *uchi* and *soto* are moving targets. They shift fluidly, depending on what we are talking about.

Japanese people often feel safe in a group setting and enjoy cooperation. That is why we excel at productivity by working well together. On the other hand, a rogue in the system stands out, and is often criticized.

A deeper look

Tetsuro Watsuji, philosopher (1889–1960), discussed *uchi* and *soto* in his work 風土 *Fuudo* [Climate and Culture]. He offered the example of how a husband and a wife in Japan refer to each other. A husband calls his wife 家内 (*kanai*, person who stays inside the house) and a wife calls her husband うちの人 (*uchi no hito*, person of the house). Watsuji did not find anything close to the Japanese concepts of *uchi* and *soto* in European languages. Social anthropologist Chie Nakane (1926–) analyzed the concepts in her book タテ社会の人間関係 *Tate Shakai no Ningen Kankei* [Japanese Society]. She pointed out that Japanese people's awareness of *uchi* and *soto* can strengthen the unity of an organization, while at the same time, exclude outsiders.

In the Japanese language, we have several expressions using *uchi* and *soto*.

❀ 内輪の事情を外に漏らす (*uchiwa no jijou o soto ni morasu*) Leak to the outside.

❀ 内弁慶 (*uchi benkei*) A person who displays a strong will and is boastful inside his group, but is reserved and weak outside of it. Benkei was a monk in the late Heian period (794–1185), who was known to have massive strength.

❀ 内祝い (*uchi iwai*) Celebrating something only within a group, such as family or close friends.

❀ 外面がいい (*sotozura ga ii*) Someone who gives attitude to members of his in-group but displays a saccharine demeanor to outsiders.

As you see, Japanese people are extremely sensitive to the line between *uchi* and *soto*. That is to say, we apply clear distinctions between people who represent inside and outside, and act accordingly. Please refer to the Chapter 1-4: けじめ (*Kejime*, Distinction) for more on this.

世間 *Seken*, Society/The World

世間 (*seken*) refers to the outside world, relative to where an individual works and lives. From the viewpoint of the individual, *seken* consists of outsiders, or people of *soto*.

The dichotomy between *uchi* and *soto* (inside and outside) [see Chapter 1-1] and the distinction between an individual and *seken* differ in vantage points. When we refer to *uchi* and *soto*, we focus on *uchi*, where we are protected by our own people. *Soto* is what is outside of *uchi*. However, when we talk about *seken* and the individual, here we focus on *seken* and the efforts individuals take to conform to it. We feel that our performance as individuals is seen and judged by *seken*. In the Japanese world, being unmindful of *seken* can be reckless.

News media use the expressions 世間の声 (*seken no koe,* voice of society) and 世間が許さない (*seken ga yurusanai*, society does not allow) to discuss political or social issues.

Example 1

そんな行動は、家族は認めても、世間が許さないだろう。
*Sonna koudou wa, kazoku wa mitomete mo, **seken** ga yurusanai darou.*
Though the family allows that kind of conduct, society will not permit it.

Example 2

たとえ世間を敵に回しても、私は自分の考えを貫きます。
*Tatoe **seken** o teki ni mawashite mo, watashi wa jibun no kangae o tsuranuki masu.*
Even if I am shunned by society, I'll stick to my principles.

Example 3

大学生にもなって、そんな世間知らずなことを言うと笑われる。

*Daigakusei ni mo natte, sonna **seken shirazu** na koto o iu to warawareru.*
Now that you're in college, people will laugh if you talk like an ignoramus.

世間知らず (***seken shirazu***, ignorant of the world) is a term to criticize a person who has not learned the rules and customs of society. Parents are expected to teach their children those rules, so if a child does not follow them, he would be considered しつけが悪い (*shitsuke ga warui*, undisciplined)[see Chapter 1-3]. Here, *seken* is distinguished from *uchi* (family), as an extension of the individual.

Japanese people generally keep *seken* in mind when deciding how to act. The Japanese language has numerous expressions using this term.

❁ 渡る世間に鬼はなし（世の中は悪い人ばかりではない）

*Wataru **seken** ni oni wa nashi.* (*Yo no naka wa warui hito bakari de wa nai.*)

The world we live in has no true demons. (Not everyone is evil; there is kindness to be found in the world.)

❁ 世間の風は冷たい（家の中は住みやすく暖かいのに対して、社会は厳しい）

Seken *no kaze wa tsumetai.* (*Ie no naka wa sumi yasuku atatakai no ni taishite, shakai wa kibishii.*)

Cold wind blows on your world. (Even if life at home is warm and cozy, society is strict and judgmental.)

❀ 世間に顔向けできない（何か悪いことをしたので、世間に対して恥ずかしい思いをする）

Seken ni kaomuke dekinai.（Nanika warui koto o sita node, seken ni taishite, hazukashii omoi o suru.）

I cannot show my face in public.（Since I committed bad deeds, I feel ashamed to face the world.）

❀ 世間体が悪い（世間の規範から外れている）

Sekentei ga warui.（Seken no kihan kara hazurete iru.）

It looks bad in society.（It deviates from the norms of society.）

As you have seen, Japanese people care much about how *seken* evaluates them or their family. Below are expressions where the actions of an individual affect the reputation of his family.

❀ 家名に傷がつく（家のメンバーの一人によって、家全体の名誉が汚される）

Kamei ni kizu ga tsuku.（Ie no menbaa no hitori ni yotte, ie zentai no meiyo ga kegasareru.）

The family name is tarnished.（Because of one family member, the honor of the entire family gets ruined.）

❀ 親の顔に泥を塗る（子どもが何か悪いことをしたため、親の名誉が汚される）

Oya no kao ni doro o nuru.（Kodomo ga nanika warui koto o shita tame, oya no meiyo ga kegasareru.）

To fling mud on the face of one's parents.（Due to a child's misdeeds, the honor of his parents is stained.）

Nowadays, the concept of *ie* (family) does not carry the weight it had in the past, but the relationship between family and *seken* still plays a leading role in the mind and actions of Japanese people.

A deeper look

The word 人間 (*ningen*, human being) is composed of two characters, 人 (*hito/nin*, person) and 間 (*aida/gen*, space between). In modern Japanese, both *ningen* and *hito/nin* have the meaning of human being, but originally, *ningen* held a distinct meaning. At first, 人間 (*ningen*) was read じんかん (*jinkan*), and it meant 人と人の間 (*hito to hito no aida*, the space between people) and 人の世 (*hito no yo*, the human world). The same word (人間) in Chinese also means 世間 (*seken*) and 世の中 (*yo no naka*, world), but does not hold the meaning of 人 (person).

So, why did we begin to use both 人間 (*ningen*) and 人 (*hito*) to indicate the same meaning in the Japanese language?

The philosopher Tetsuro Watsuji (1889–1960) focused on this question. In his work, 人間の学としての倫理学 *Ningen no Gaku to Shite no Rinrigaku* [Ethics as the Study of Man], he offers an etymological analysis of the word 人間 (*ningen*). By underlining the dual nature of the human being, as a unique individual and as a social being, he explains that an individual can ultimately be defined as a 人 (*hito*, person) when he establishes a connection to society. Therefore, the Japanese word 人間 (*ningen*) indicates a person (人 *nin*) who lives in the spaces between (間 *gen*) people of the world (世間 *seken*).

しつけ Shitsuke, Discipline

1-3

In Japan, we believe that it is the duty of parents to teach 礼儀 (*reigi*, manners) [see Chapter 4-3] to their children from an early age, so they can act properly with 外 (*soto*, outside of the family). That instruction is called しつけ (***shitsuke***, discipline).

Japanese parents educate their children using the following expressions.

❀ ちゃんとあいさつをしなさい

Chanto aisatsu o shi nasai.

Greet people properly.

❀ 悪いことをしたら、素直に「ごめんなさい」と言いなさい

Warui koto o shitara, sunao ni "gomen nasai" to ii nasai.

If you do something wrong, just say, "I'm sorry."

❀ 年上の人には丁寧な言葉を使いなさい

Toshiue no hito ni wa teinei na kotoba o tsukai nasai.

Use polite language to your elders.

❀ 人の迷惑になることをしてはいけません

Hito no meiwaku ni naru koto o shite wa ike masen.

Do not make trouble with others.

❀ わがままばかり言っていないで、がまんしなさい

Wagamama bakari itte inaide, gaman shi nasai.

You should keep quiet and stop being so self-centered.

As shown above, Japanese parents teach their children how to behave in society. In most cases, if a child shows bad manners or attitude, we do not think it is the child's problem. Rather, we presume that the parents are failing to discipline the child.

Example 1

最近の子どもがきちんとあいさつできないのは、親の**しつけが悪い**からだ。

*Saikin no kodomo ga kichinto aisatsu dekinai no wa, oya no **shitsuke ga warui** kara da.*

Children cannot greet people properly these days because of a lack of discipline at home.

Example 2

小さい頃、食べ物を残してはいけないと、祖母に厳しく**しつけられました**。

*Chiisai koro, tabemono o nokoshite wa ikenai to, sobo ni kibishiku **shitsukerare mashita**.*

When I was little, my grandmother was always strict about finishing my plate.

We use the expression 親のしつけが悪い (*oya no shitsuke ga warui*, weak discipline by parents) not only for children, but also for college students and even adults. Though a child in Western culture is considered independent when reaching adulthood, parents in Japan must share some responsibility for their offspring at any age. That philosophy relates to the concept of *uchi to soto* [see Chapter 1-1]. 家 (*ie*) or *uchi* is the base from which we educate a person to live in *seken/soto*. Therefore, a person's actions in *soto* originate from *uchi*.

We often use the expressions such as 親の顔が見たい (*oya no kao ga mi tai*, I want to see his parents' face) and お里が知れる (*osato ga shireru*, to reveal the family background). Both attribute a person's misdeeds to the result of 家でのしつけが悪い (*ie de no shitsuke ga warui*, poor discipline at home).

Example 3

こんな常識を知らないなんて、どんな育て方をしたんだ。親の顔が見たいよ。

Konna joushiki o shiranai nante, donna sodatekata o shitan da. Oya no kao ga mi tai yo.

That guy has no common sense. What kind of parents raised him? I'd love to see their face.

Example 4

どんなにいい服を着ていても、話し方や食べ方でその人のお里が知れる。

Donna ni ii fuku o kite ite mo, hanashikata ya tabekata de sono hito no osato ga shireru.

Even wearing nice clothes, her way of talking and eating reveals her true background.

The word *shitsuke*（discipline）is also used to talk about the training of employees and domestic animals.

Example 5

隣の犬はいつも夜中に吠えてうるさい。飼い主がちゃんと**しつけ**をしていないのだろう。

*Tonari no inu wa itsumo yonaka ni hoete urusai. Kainushi ga chanto **shitsuke** o shite inai no darou.*

The neighbor's dog always barks at night. They're probably not training him.

Example 6

この会社は社員の**しつけが悪い**。客が来てもあいさつもしない。

*Kono kaisha wa shain no **shitsuke ga warui**. Kyaku ga kite mo aisatsu mo shinai.*

The employees of this company are not well-disciplined. They don't even greet their guests.

In example 6, it is the responsibility of the company to train employees. Here, we believe that the company is *uchi* and the guests are *soto*. It is a prime example of how Japanese people distinguish *uchi* and *soto* [see Chapter 1-1].

When we make clothes, we use basting threads to mark the fabric before sewing, so that the sewing lines are neat. That way, we can ensure a fine product. The use of basting threads is called *shitsuke*. In the same way, we call family education *shitsuke*, so children follow the proper lines to live in society.

Shitsuke is written as 躾 in *kanji*. The character is composed of 身 (body/self) and 美 (beauty). As such, it indicates the embellishment or enrichment of self. Japanese *kanji* characters were originally borrowed from China, but there are some *kanji* that originated in Japan, and they are called 国字 (*kokuji*, country characters). 躾 is one of them. We see the sensitive mind of the Japanese, in creating the concept of *shitsuke* (discipline) and the character 躾 (*shitsuke*, enrichment of self).

けじめ *Kejime*, Distinction

One of the most valued concepts held by Japanese people is けじめ (*kejime*, distinction). *Kejime* is a clear distinction between things. It designates our attitude and actions, which we change depending on time, place, or occasion, and in relation to other people. We can see *kejime* everywhere in daily life.

For example, foreigners might be struck by the swift changes in department store displays. Entire Christmas trees are suddenly swapped to *kadomatsu* (traditional Japanese pine decorations for New Year's Day) by December 26, whereas in other countries, Christmas decoration can last well into January. This shows how earnestly Japanese people embrace the power of *kejime*.

From childhood, we are told けじめのある行動をしなさい (***kejime** no aru koudou o shi nasai*, behave in a serious manner by drawing a clear line, pay attention to what you should be doing).

Example 1

勉強するときは勉強する、遊ぶときは遊ぶ。けじめのある生活をしなさい。

Benkyou suru toki wa benkyou suru, asobu toki wa asobu. ***Kejime*** *no aru seikatsu o shi nasai.*

When it is time to study, study. When it is time to play, play. Keep that line clear in life.

Example 2

あの二人は仕事中もおしゃべりばかりしていて、公私のけじめがない。

*Ano futari wa shigoto chuu mo oshaberi bakari shite ite, koushi no **kejime** ga nai.*

Those two keep chatting at work. They don't separate work from private life.

Japanese people adjust their attitude and manner of speaking depending on the situation. This is called けじめをつける (***kejime o tsukeru***, to draw a line). Even if one is talking to his close friend or lover, he must use honorifics at work and treat that person as a colleague. If he speaks casually or discusses private life with her at work, he gives a bad impression to his other colleagues. He would be labeled as a person lacking *kejime* (a person who cannot draw a line between private and public life).

It is crucial in Japan to draw a clear line in relationship to others. People must change their attitude or manner of speaking by considering their relationship to the listener, including hierarchy, gender, and affiliation (whether the listener belongs to *uchi* or *soto*). If a colleague is promoted over us, we must start using honorific speech and show respect. Some might think a friend is always a friend, but we still need to employ *kejime* in consideration of time and place. In Japanese society, drawing a line in official settings would not harm a close relationship between friends. Rather, it shows respect for that person.

A deeper look

The concept of *kejime* is likely the most important element controlling conduct in Japanese society. As you have seen, *kejime* involves the distinction and differentiation between states of being, but those states are wide-ranging. By being sensitive to the many distinctions in life, such as *uchi* and *soto*, man and woman, superior and subordinate, senior and junior, teacher and student, etc., one can apply the proper language and attitude to the situation.

From childhood, Japanese people are used to hearing things like, "You are the eldest brother, so behave this way." At school, we are admonished, "You should not use such language to your teacher or your seniors!" Once we enter a company, we learn again how to speak and act appropriately with our superiors and clients. It is imperative for us to be aware of *kejime* at home, school, and the workplace, and if we cannot demonstrate the appropriate conduct, we will be criticized as けじめがない (*kejime ga nai*, not knowing where to draw the line) and だらしがない (*darashi ga nai*, undisciplined).

素直 *Sunao*, Obedience and Innocence

素直 (*sunao*) in Japanese means being purely yourself. It describes someone whose heart is in the right place and who is not twisted.

Originally, Japanese people tend to think that something natural and undisturbed by humans has more value. We prefer the simple and plain to the overembellished. For that reason, the *sunao* personality is highly valued.

Example 1

あの子は素直で、とてもいい子だね。

*Ano ko wa **sunao** de, totemo ii ko da ne.*
That child is obedient and innocent. He truly is a good child.

Young children normally do not doubt people nor try to make themselves look good. If a child listens to adults without talking back, he could be praised with, "He has a child's innocence," or "He's a good kid." On the other hand, if a child doubts the things adults say or talks back to his parents, people will think he is not *sunao*, not pure.

Sunao is also an essential quality in adults.

Example 2

自分がやったと素直に認めなさい。

*Jibun ga yatta to **sunao** ni mitome nasai.*
Just honestly admit that you did it yourself.

Example 3

上司の指示に**素直**に従う。

*Joushi no shiji ni **sunao** ni shitagau.*
Dutifully follow the instructions of your superior.

The word *sunao* indicates that a person's heart is not twisted, but in Example 2 and Example 3, it is used to designate obedience and uprightness [see Chapter 7-5].

Example 4

彼は人の言うことを**素直**に受け取らないので、話していて疲れる。

*Kare wa hito no iu koto o **sunao** ni uketoranai node, hanashite ite tsukareru.*
I'm tired of talking to him. He just questions everything.

A contrary person who doubts everything he hears is called へそ曲がり (***heso magari***, bellybutton twisted off center, perverse). *Heso* (bellybutton) is at the center of the body, so when a person's *heso* is not in the right place, his character is crooked.

甘える *Amaeru,* To Rely on Another's Love or Kindness

甘える (*amaeru*) is a verb describing the attitude and actions of a person who leans on people's kindness or goodwill, especially with an assumption of caring or the expectation of help by others.

The prime example is the conduct of a child who presumes his parents will take care of him unconditionally. A baby naturally clings to his mother or cries to seek her love. These are expressions of *amae* (dependence, the expectation to be loved and cared for). Even when an older child cries and pleads with his mother to get him something, that is considered *amae*.

If a parent allows her child to do whatever he likes and gives him anything he wants, the action of the parent is called 甘やかす (*amayakasu,* to spoil). If a parent spoils a child, it naturally creates a willful child (a child who thinks he is the center of the world). From the viewpoint of *shitsuke* [see Chapter 1-3], spoiling a child is considered a failure of parenting.

Example 1

赤ちゃんが母親に甘える姿はかわいい。

*Akachan ga hahaoya ni **amaeru** sugata wa kawaii.*

Babies look adorable when they cling to their mother.

Example 2

あの子は欲しいものは何でも両親に買ってもらうなど、甘やかされて育った。

*Ano ko wa hoshii mono wa nandemo ryoushin ni katte morau nado, **amayakasarete sodatta**.*

That child's parents bought him anything he wanted. He was raised to be a brat.

When we think of *amaeru*, we picture it with a young child, but we often see *amaeru* with adults.

If a girl pleads with her lover, "Honey, please buy me a diamond ring," this comes from her *amae* attitude. If a company employee gets in trouble and presumes his superiors will bail him out, that way of thinking is also considered *amae*. *Amae* embodies the feeling of expectations fulfilled by people in a close relationship. Japanese people easily rely on each other, because we assume people of *uchi* are always there for us [see Chapter 1-1]. Also, we expect them to read our true thoughts [see Chapter 3-4].

However, as adults, we are more likely to see *amae* as bad behavior. If a person leans too heavily on others for help and believes they will always forgive and forget, that is too much *amae*. We can use the proverb 親しき仲にも礼儀あり (*shitashiki naka ni mo reigi ari*, good manners even between friends, good fences make good neighbors) to educate him. Sometimes, it would be better to hold an attitude of 遠慮 (*enryo*, hesitation of self-expression) [see Chapter 3-1] and decline offers of help.

Now, if a person keeps avoiding *amae* by declining offers of kindness, even after becoming close, that is called 水くさい (***mizu kusai***, watery and tasteless; distant).

Example 3

A よかったら、お昼、うちで食べていきませんか。

Yokattara, ohiru, uchi de tabete iki masen ka.

If it's all right, why don't you stay for lunch?

B えっ、いいんですか。それでは、遠慮なく、お言葉に甘えさせていただきます。

E, iin desu ka? Soredewa, enryo naku, okotoba ni amaesasete itadaki masu.

Really? Is that OK? In that case, I won't decline your kind offer.

Here, B did not want to overdue *enryo* by declining, so he did *amae* by accepting A's kindness. Though difficult, it is critical to skillfully balance *amae* and *enryo* to maintain good relationships with others in Japan.

Psychoanalyst Takeo Doi (1920–2009) is known for writing about *amae* in his treatise, 「甘え」の構造 *"Amae" no Kouzou* [The Anatomy of Dependence]. Although he witnessed the behavior and actions of *amae* during his research in the United States, he noticed that Western culture lacked the concept of *amae* and had no vocabulary to describe it. He assumed that people in the Western world were not conscious of *amae*. On the other hand, in Japanese society, *amae* is common in daily life, and the term is widely used. Doi concluded that the concept of *amae* is uniquely Japanese. The book created a sensation in Japan, becoming a bestseller.

In his book, Doi explains that *amaeru* is the feeling of desire to become one with another person, and it is clear that the psyche of *amae* has a strong causative function in Japanese life.

Everyday Conversations 1: Greeting, Farewell, and Gratitude

いってらっしゃい（***itterasshai***, go and come back safely, have a good day）

Conversation between neighbors in the morning:

伊藤： おはようございます。
Itou: *Ohayou gozaimasu.*
　　　 Good morning.

山田： おはようございます。
Yamada: *Ohayou gozaimasu.*
　　　 Good morning.

伊藤： 今日は寒いですね。
Itou: *Kyou wa samui desu ne.*
　　　 It's cold today, isn't it?

山田： そうですね。すっかり冬ですね。
Yamada: *Sou desu ne. Sukkari fuyu desu ne.*
　　　 Yes. It's already winter, you know.

伊藤： これからお仕事ですか。
Itou: *Kore kara oshigoto desu ka.*
　　　 Are you on the way to work?

山田： ええ。
Yamada: *Ee.*
　　　 Yeah.

伊藤： お気をつけて。**いってらっしゃい。**
Itou: *Oki o tsukete.* ***Itterasshai.***
　　　 Ok, take care. See you later (Go and return safely).

山田：　**いってきます。**

Yamada:　***Itte ki masu***.

　　　　I'll be going now (I'll go and come back).

The above dialogue is a typical conversation between Japanese neighbors in the morning. They do not say anything important, but with this kind of small talk, Japanese people can begin the day with a feeling of goodwill. We express the wish that the person returns safely from *soto* (outside) to *uchi* (home) **[see Chapter 1-1]** instead of offering a simple goodbye.

Even within their company, employees use the same set of expressions, confirming that they are all part of *uchi* (comrades at work). When we first see our boss or coworkers in the morning, we habitually say おはようございます (*ohayou gozaimasu*, good morning). Greetings are a necessity in Japanese society. If we said nothing, they might think we are sick or that we hold some kind of grudge towards them. If we greeted someone and he did not respond, we would worry and try to figure out what is wrong.

We also use set expressions of gratitude before and after eating. いただきます (*itadaki masu*, I humbly receive this meal, thank you for this food before me) precedes the meal, and ごちそうさま (*gochisousama*, I appreciate your efforts to provide food to me, thank you for the food I ate) follows the meal. These expressions demonstrate our gratefulness to the people who provided food, and then gratitude after the meal for having treated us. Japanese people have been trained to use these expressions since childhood **[see Chapter 1-3]**, and most people say them without a thought. These expressions can hold layered meanings, such as gratitude to the farmer who grew the rice and to the fisherman who provided his catch, and more directly, to the person who cooked or who paid for the meal. *Itadaki masu* also signals that we will commence eating, and *gochisousama* indicates that we are finished.

Every country has different forms of greeting, but Japanese people put extra importance on salutations. We could talk only about the season or the weather, but it is important to have some sort of exchange to greet people or bid them farewell. These exchanges demonstrate our appreciation of daily life and the importance of fostering relationships with others.

Chapter 2

他人の目を意識する

Tanin no Me o Ishiki Suru
To Be Mindful of the Public Eye

人目 *Hitome,* Public Eye/Perception by Others

Japanese people are known to be sensitive to 恥 (*haji*, shame) [see Chapter 2-2]. The emotion 恥ずかしい (*hazukashii*, ashamed, embarrassed) and the concept of *haji* are products of our overt attention on other people's perception of us, be it actions or attitude. It is not an exaggeration to say that we live in fear of what others think of us. Here, "others" refers more specifically to the people of *seken* (society) [see Chapter 1-2]. The viewpoint from people surrounding us is called 人目 (*hitome*, people's eye, perception by others).

Example 1

彼女に話しかけたかったけど、人目が気になって、できなかった。

Kanojo ni hanashikake takatta kedo, ***hitome*** *ga ki ni natte, dekinakatta.*

Though I did want to talk to her, I just couldn't. How would it look?

Example 2

犯罪は人目のない所で行われることが多い。

Hanzai wa ***hitome*** *no nai tokoro de okonawareru koto ga ooi.*

People are more likely to commit crimes behind closed doors.

Foreigners in Japan may be puzzled by the many silent passengers on the train. We are acutely aware of *hitome* in public and try to avoid bringing undue attention on ourselves.

The number of Japanese expressions related to **hitome** shows how important this concept is to us.

❁ 彼は母親の葬式のとき、**人目もはばからずに**大声で泣いた。

Kare wa hahaoya no soushiki no toki, ***hitome mo habakarazu ni*** *oogoe de naita.*
At his mother's funeral, heedless of the others, he cried loudly.

❁ このポスターをどこか、**人目につく**場所に貼っておいて。

Kono posutaa o dokoka, ***hitome ni tsuku*** *basho ni hatte oite.*
Post this flyer where people will notice.

❁ 彼はいつも**人目をひく**ような派手な服を着ている。

Kare wa itsumo ***hitome o hiku*** *you na hade na fuku o kite iru.*
He always wears flashy clothes to grab people's attention.

❁ 会社を首になったが、**人目がうるさい**から、毎朝、出勤するふりをしている。

Kaisha o kubi ni natta ga, ***hitome ga urusai*** *kara, maiasa, shukkin suru furi o shite iru.*

Though my company fired me, I just pretend to go to work every morning to avoid undue attention.

❁ 電車の中で平気で抱き合うなど、今の若い人の行動には**人目に余る**ものがある。

Densha no naka de heiki de dakiau nado, ima no wakai hito no koudou ni wa ***hitome ni amaru*** *mono ga aru.*

What young people do these days, like openly cuddling in the train—it's offensive.

❀ 犯罪者の家族は、**人目を避ける**ようにして生活している。

*Hanzaisha no kazoku wa, **hitome o sakeru** you ni shite seikatsu shite iru.*

The families of criminals spend their entire lives avoiding the public eye.

❀ 昔の恋人たちは、**人目を忍ぶ**ようにして会っていたものですよ。

*Mukashi no koibitotachi wa, **hitome o shinobu** you ni shite atte ita mono desu yo.*

To meet, lovers in old Japan had to sneak by prying eyes.

❀ 二人は、**人目を盗んで**、密会を重ねていた。

*Futari wa, **hitome o nusunde**, mikkai o kasanete ita.*

By ducking the public eye, those two repeatedly held secret rendezvouses.

As you see above, the Japanese social psyche keeps us alert to the views of people around us, and to the eyes of *seken*.

It is undeniable that Japanese people go through life acutely conscious of the gaze of others, and we have abundant expressions involving *hitome*. In fact, we see expressions of *hitome* in Japan's oldest anthology of *waka* (classical Japanese poetry), 万葉集 *Man'yōshū* [Collection of Ten Thousand Leaves].

❀ うつせみの**人目**繁けば　ぬばたまの夜の夢にを継ぎて　見えこそ

*Utsusemi no **hitome** shigekeba nubatama no yoru no yume ni o tsugite mie koso*

There are too many eyes on us to meet in person. In the darkness of night, please keep appearing in my dreams.

❀ うつせみの人目を繁み　石橋の間近き君に　恋わたるかも

*Utsusemi no **hitome** o shigemi iwahashi no majikaki kimi ni koi wataru kamo*

With so many eyes watching, though you are so close, I cannot meet you. It makes me miss you even more.

❀ かくばかり面影にのみ念おえば　如何にかもせん　人目繁くて

*Kakubakari omokage ni nomi omooeba ikani kamo sen **hitome** shigekute*

Though your visage keeps appearing in my mind, it is painful for me not to see you in person. The meddling public will not let us alone.

The 万葉集（*Man'yōshū*）is a compendium of ancient poetry compiled in the late 8th century. It contains 4,500 poems in 20 volumes, representing all social classes, from the lowest ranks to nobility and the imperial family. From these poems, we see that to live and fall in love, Japanese people have been struggling with *hitome* from ancient times.

恥 *Haji,* Shame

In life, we occupy various roles and positions in society. In Japan, each person is evaluated by *seken*（society）[see Chapter 1-2], so we go through life seeing our value in society assessed by others.

If one commits a visible crime, a social blunder, or reveals improper behavior, his reputation will be diminished. His pride will be hurt and his honor damaged. We call the feeling 恥ずかしい（***hazukashii***, ashamed, embarrassed）.

We have various expressions describing this emotion, such as 格好がつかない（*kakkou ga tsukanai*, the important look is not attached, look bad to people）, 世間体が悪い（*sekentei ga warui*, look bad in society）, 面目がない（*menboku ga nai*, no face nor eyes, to have no honor）, 面子がつぶれる（*mentsu ga tsubureru*, face is crushed, to lose face）. They are all the result of 恥をかく（***haji o kaku***, to disgrace oneself）.

Example 1

彼女を食事に誘ったのに、財布を忘れて**恥をかいた**。

*Kanojo o shokuji ni sasotta noni, saifu o wasurete **haji o kaita**.*

I took my girlfriend out to dinner, but I forgot my wallet and was totally humiliated.

In Example 1, instead of saying he felt embarrassed（恥ずかしかった, *hazukashikatta*）, he said he was humiliated（恥をかいた, *haji o kaita*）, because he was worried about losing face in front of his girlfriend and the people at the restaurant. The adjective 恥ずかしい（*hazukashii*）describes a personal feeling of embarrassment, whereas 恥をかく (*haji o kaku*) indicates that the mishap is known to others.

Say, if you were to slip carelessly and fall. You might feel 恥ずかしい (*hazukashii*), even if nobody saw it, but you could not use 恥をかく (*haji o kaku*). **Haji** is not born out of personal feelings, rather from the awareness of public disdain (the eyes of *seken* [see Chapter 1-2]) or the threat that one's moral reputation could be ruined.

Japanese people are constantly wary of the public eye. We feel the weight of *haji* intensely. Conversely, we condemn those who are unconcerned with *haji* or commit misdeeds without qualms.

Example 2

お金のために友人を裏切るなんて、君はなんという恥知らずな人間だ。

*Okane no tame ni yuujin o uragiru nante, kimi wa nanto iu **haji shirazu** na ningen da.*
You betrayed your own friend for money. You are a worthless bastard (shameless human being).

恥を知る (*haji o shiru*, to know shame) is vital to living in Japanese society with dignity. 恥知らず (*haji shirazu*, do not know *haji*, shameless) is a powerfully damaging expression regarding one's character, but there are other softer expressions, such as みっともない (***mittomonai***, want to look away, unseemly) and 見苦しい (***migurushii***, hard to see, despicable). These adjectives can modify a look or a behavior, such as みっともない格好 (*mittomonai kakkou*, indecent appearance) and 見苦しい態度 (*migurushii taido*, contemptable attitude). Still, like *haji*, these expressions speak to the harm done to us in the public eye, rather than to our own hurt feelings.

Example 3

そんな汚れた服を着て、みっともないからすぐ脱ぎなさい。
Sonna yogoreta fuku o kite, mittomonai kara sugu nugi nasai.
Those clothes are filthy. Take them off right now, before anyone sees you.

Example 3 is a common expression for Japanese parents. They fear that a bad image of their child could harm their own reputation.

American anthropologist Ruth Benedict (1887–1948) wrote *The Chrysanthemum and the Sword*, a broad study of Japanese behavior and social customs. In the book, she labeled Japanese culture as 恥の文化 (*haji no bunka*, culture of shame) and illustrated how, for Japanese people, *haji* is a potent coercive force to follow social norms and maintain honor.

A deeper look

The perception of *haji* varies depending on the era and social rank.

From the mid-Heian period (794–1185), the life of the *bushi* (warriors) was predetermined from birth. They fought for their master and liege, gained booty, and safeguarded their clan. If they were the first to attack the enemy base and fight bravely, that was called 一番乗り (***ichiban nori***, the first ride, the first to arrive). That was considered the highest honor as a warrior.

Conversely, conduct without bravery was condemned as 武士の恥 (*bushi no haji*, warrior's shame). In the battlefield, 敵に背中を見せる (***teki ni senaka o miseru***, show one's back to the enemy) signified cowardice, which was thought to be the lowest form of *haji*. In particular, 後ろ傷 (***ushiro kizu***, back cut) was considered the worst form of *haji*. Being cut on the back, instead of the front, gave proof of fearing and fleeing the enemy.

During the Edo period (1603–1868), the constant threat of war was effectively eliminated. Thus, the primary identity of the warriors was lost, and they had to figure out what to do with themselves in peacetime. Codes of conduct were developed, called 武士道 (***bushidou***, the way of the warrior) [see Chapter 6-5]. The codes laid out their ethical values in detail. A warrior should be ready to sacrifice his life for his master, even in peaceful times, which is a part of 忠の考え方 (*chuu no kangaekata*, loyalty code). A warrior should not be afraid of death. A warrior should not desire wealth. The codes exemplified the virtue of the warrior class. For warriors, to lose their honor was to bear extreme *haji*. In that sense, from the viewpoint of *bushidou* perfection, the warriors of ancient times should have incurred *haji* to fight for property and booty.

Over the 700 years of Japanese rule by *bushi*, the perception of *haji* within *bushidou* evolved to the codes of conduct central to Japanese society, and is still potent today.

照れる　*Tereru*, To Be Abashed

How would you respond if somebody told you, "Your tie is chic," or "Your wife is lovely"?

People might reply, "Thank you," or "I think so, too." However, most Japanese people will look embarrassed and come back with "No, it's not so nice," or "No, not really." We tend to react awkwardly to compliments, followed by a rather sheepish denial. This attitude is called 照れる (***tereru***, to show shyness or be abashed).

Why do we get embarrassed when receiving a compliment?

Normally, we consider it inappropriate to openly express our feelings. If we do, it would be regarded as はしたない (*hashitanai*, ill-mannered) [see Chapter 7-1]. Consequently, we shy away from strong emotions, whether happy or sad.

Of course, we naturally feel delighted to receive a compliment. Yet, at the same time, we feel embarrassed to show a happy face. That confused feeling is called 照れくさい (***terekusai***, embarrassed or awkward). In Japan, we can be embarrassed both by humiliating and joyous situations. Making a mistake in public makes us feel 恥ずかしい (*hazukashii*, ashamed and embarrassed) [see Chapter 2-2], but being praised in public makes us feel 照れくさい (*terekusai*).

Example 1

そんなに褒められたら、照れるなあ。

*Sonna ni homeraretara, **tereru** naa.*

Stop laying on praise like that. Now I'm self-conscious.

Example 2

あちらのきれいな方は奥様ですか。照れないで紹介してくださいよ。

Achira no kirei na kata wa okusama desu ka. **Terenaide** *shoukai shite kudasai yo.*

That gorgeous creature over there—is that your wife? Would you introduce us, without getting all gawky about it?

When someone says 奥さん、きれいですね (*okusan, kirei desu ne*, your wife is a beauty, you know), and you respond いやあ、照れるなあ (*iyaa, tereru naa*, oh, I am so embarrassed), it means that you admit it. Here, the underlying meaning is, "I think so myself, but I can't say it, because I am too embarrassed."

Traditionally, *bushi* (warriors) were supposed to hide their emotions. Because of that, it seems that there are many 照れ屋 (*tereya*, people who easily get embarrassed and shy) among Japanese men. A Japanese man might not openly express endearment to his lover or praise his family in front of others. It does not indicate a lack of love for them. Rather, he just feels it would be awkward to express it in public.

Both *tereru* and *hazukashii* indicate the feeling of embarrassment, but きまり悪い (**kimariwarui**, embarrassed silly) indicates a more confused state. *Kimariwarui* is composed of *kimari* (decision) and *warui* (bad). Here, you are at a loss on how to react. Say you cried while watching a movie with a friend, and you got embarrassed when the friend noticed. You would feel *kimariwarui* because you had no idea how to handle the situation. The friend might have the same feeling!

People from other cultures, where the display of emotions is natural, might find it odd that Japanese people get embarrassed when receiving compliments.

A deeper look

Japanese people clearly differentiate between *uchi* and *soto* [see Chapter 1-1] and make efforts not to reveal information about *uchi* (family) to *soto* (the outside world). Though we might broach the topic, we are not supposed to brag openly about our families.

For that reason, when someone asks us about our family, we tend to speak about them humbly or in a bad light. In fact, when someone praises a family member, we are likely to respond negatively.

✿ A お宅のお子さんは、とても勉強ができるそうですね。

Otaku no okosan wa, totemo benkyou ga dekiru sou desu ne.
I heard that your child is a stellar student.

B いやいや、どら息子で、困ってるんですよ。

Iyaiya, doramusuko de, komatterun desu yo.
No, no. That good-for-nothing son of ours only gives us problems.

✿ A 奥さんは、絵がお上手だそうですね。

Okusan wa, e ga ojouzu da sou desu ne.
I heard that your wife is a talented painter.

B とんでもない、うちのやつのなんて、幼稚園のお絵かき程度ですよ。

Tondemonai, uchi no yatsu no nante, youchien no oekaki teido desu yo.
No way! The woman draws like it's kindergarten.

We even have expressions to describe this misrepresentation. 照れ笑い (***terewarai***, embarrassed grin) is used to hide our genuine feelings. When we laugh off or shrug off our feeling of embarrassment, it is called 照れ隠し (***terekakushi***, hide one's embarrassment). 照れる (*tereru*) is a characteristic Japanese emotion.

Chapter 3
周囲に配慮する
Shuui ni Hairyo Suru
To Consider the People around Us

遠慮 *Enryo*, Restraint

At its core, 遠慮 (*enryo*) means being thoughtful with respect to the situation or to avoid inconvenience to others. However, when we use the verb 遠慮する (*enryo suru*, to decline something humbly), it means that we refrain from acting after carefully examining the situation.

Example 1

先輩にすぐ連絡をとりたかったが、深夜だったので、電話するのは遠慮した。

*Senpai ni sugu renraku o tori takatta ga, shin'ya datta node, denwa suru no wa **enryo shita**.*

Though I wanted to contact my senior right away, I thought it better not to call late at night.

Example 2

上司 今晩、X君と飲みに行くけど、君も来ないか？
Joushi *Konban, X-kun to nomi ni iku kedo, kimi mo konai ka?*
Superior I'm going out drinking with X tonight. Care to join us?

部下 すみません。今日はちょっと、遠慮しておきます。
Buka *Sumi masen. Kyou wa chotto, **enryo shite** oki masu.*
Subordinate Sorry. I'll pass on it this time (for your sake).

遠慮します (*enryo shi masu*, I'll pass) is commonly used when we decline invitations. The message is that, in consideration of others, we choose not to participate. Though in practice, we can use the term to soften the fact that we really do not want to do it.

Example 3

A さあ、どうぞ**遠慮なく**召し上がってください。
*Saa, douzo **enryo naku** meshiagatte kudasai.*
Please don't worry and start your meal.

B すみません。それでは、**遠慮なく**いただきます。
*Sumi masen. Soredewa, **enryo naku** itadaki masu.*
Thank you. Then, I will be happy to do so.

If a person we do not know well offers us a gift, we usually decline politely. But if he insists, we may accept it, saying それでは遠慮なく (*soredewa enryo naku*, All right, then. I'll accept it without reservation).

Hence, when we offer something to someone, we use どうぞ遠慮なく (*douzo enryo naku*, please do it without reservation) to allow the person the freedom to accept it. In Japanese society, before making an offer of kindness, we try to relieve the recipient's pressure to decline.

Example 4

あの人はとても**遠慮深くて**、好感が持てる。
*Ano hito wa totemo **enryo bukakute**, koukan ga moteru.*
That person exercises solid self-control, which lends a good impression.

Example 5

初対面でプライベートな質問ばかりするのは**無遠慮過ぎる**。
*Shotaimen de puraibeeto na shitsumon bakari suru no wa **buenryo** sugiru.*
At first meeting, to ask only private questions is impudent.

遠慮深い人 (*enryo bukai hito*, a person with deep restraint) can be used to praise people who are 控えめ (*hikaeme*, restrained) [see Chapter 5-1] and act humbly. On the other hand, 遠慮のない人 (*enryo no nai hito*, an unrestrained person) or 無遠慮な人 (*buenryo na hito*, an unfettered/brusque person) are objectionable. ずうずうしい (*zuuzuushii*, impudent, shameless) or あつかましい (*atsukamashii*, brazen, pushy) are similar to *buenryo*.

Example 6

人のものを勝手に食べるなんて**ずうずうしい**。遠慮ってものを知らないの？

*Hito no mono o katte ni taberu nante **zuuzuushii**. Enryo tte mono o shiranai no?*
You've got some nerve eating somebody else's food without asking. Can't you control yourself?

Knowingly causing trouble by getting in the way or by asking annoying favors is referred to as ずうずうしい (*zuuzuushii*) or あつかましい (*atsukamashii*) [see Chapter 1-6].

Enryo is a primary factor to sustain good relationships in Japan. Even among close friends, it is important to be considerate of each other's situation before taking action [see Chapter 1-6].

Example 7

ここでタバコを吸うのはご**遠慮**ください。

*Koko de tabako o suu no wa **goenryo kudasai**.*
Kindly refrain from smoking in this area.

ここでタバコを吸うのは
ご遠慮ください

We often see this kind of sign in public areas. ご遠慮ください (*goenryo kudasai*, please refrain from doing something) is meant to indicate XXX しないでください (XXX *shinaide kudasai*, please do not do...). The usage seems incorrect, since 遠慮する (*enryo suru*) primarily means that we refrain from doing something in consideration of others' feelings. According to that, it would be strange to ask people to do *enryo*, because *enryo* should come from each individual naturally. Here, we use the expression to soften the impact of a declaration of public policy or if a business wishes to convey a restriction to their clients.

遠慮 (*enryo*) embodies the Japanese sensitivity to be considerate of other people [see Chapter 3-2].

The word 遠慮 (*enryo*) originally meant 遠い将来まで見通す (*tooi shourai made mitoosu*, to foresee the remote future) in Chinese. In 論語 *Rongo* [The Analects of Confucius], a collection of the teachings and thoughts of Confucius, we find a saying related to *enryo*.

❀ 遠き慮りなければ必ず近き憂えあり

Tooki omonpakari nakereba kanarazu chikaki uree ari

If a man is not farsighted, then trouble is impending.

The word, 遠慮 (*enryo*), was introduced to the Japanese language as a forewarning, but, nowadays, the meaning moved closer to 配慮 (*hairyo*, consideration). We need to consider the thoughts of other people and work to avoid discourteous actions for any given situation, so we tend to defer to the people around us. In other cultures, this attitude might be criticized as 消極的 (*shoukyoku teki*, passive). However, an attitude that is 積極的 (*sekkyoku teki*, active, aggressive) is seen as 無遠慮 (*buenryo*, shameless, wantonly, selfish) from a Japanese perspective.

Because the term 遠慮 (*enryo*) captures the philosophy of consideration for others, it serves as a lubricant to reduce friction in the lives of Japanese people.

気をつかう *Ki o Tsukau*, To Be Concerned

気をつかう (*ki o tsukau*, to use mental energy, to pay attention to another's needs) is to attend to the person you are accompanying, making sure that he is not uncomfortable. Japanese people customarily think about the feelings of others, and take actions and use special language [see Chapter 2-1].

Example 1

A これ、旅行のおみやげです。どうぞ。
Kore, ryokou no omiyage desu. Douzo.
This is a small present from my trip. Please accept it.

B すみません、気をつかっていただいて…
*Sumi masen, **ki o tsukatte** itadaite...*
Thank you. Sorry that you troubled yourself on my behalf.

In Example 1, B said 気をつかっていただいて (***ki o tsukatte** itadaite*, you were so kind to think about me) to acknowledge that A worried about him. すみません (*sumi masen*) is a very common expression of apology and of gratitude, and is also used to get someone's attention. In Example 1, B says *sumi masen* both to apologize for making A worry and to thank A for his concern.

おみやげ (*omiyage*) are usually translated as "souvenir" in English. However, unlike souvenirs, *omiyage* is never bought for ourselves; they are only gifts for others. When returning from a trip, we almost always bring *omiyage* for our family, friends, and colleagues. We feel regret that we were not able to travel with them, so we show that concern in a gift. Then, the person who receives the *omiyage* apologizes for the concern. The next time that person takes a trip, he will in turn bring back *omiyage*, which also serves as repayment-in-kind for what he has received. We continue this gift exchange, back and forth, almost as an obligation.

おみやげ文化 (*omiyage bunka*, culture of gift-giving) comes out of concern for others by both the giver and the receiver. *Omiyage* shops are a major industry in Japan and are widespread in and around train stations and tourist spots.

As you have seen, Japanese people go through life concerned about other people, but pay special attention to the feeling of a superior or a person of *soto* [see Chapter 1-1].

Example 2

会議の席で社長が間違ったことを言ったが、みんな気をつかって気がつかないふりをした。

*Kaigi no seki de shachou ga machigatta koto o itta ga, minna **ki o tsukatte** ki ga tsukanai furi o shita.*

Our CEO misspoke at the meeting, but, out of concern for his feelings, everyone pretended not to notice.

Example 3

お客さんに気をつかいながら食べる豪華な接待の料理よりも、家族と気軽に食べる食事のほうがおいしい。

*Okyakusan ni **ki o tsukai** nagara taberu gouka na settai no ryouri yori mo, kazoku to kigaru ni taberu shokuji no hou ga oishii.*

A relaxed meal with family tastes better than a sumptuous business dinner spent fawning over a client.

Growing weary focusing too much on others is called 気疲れ (*kizukare*, mental fatigue). It is necessary to pay attention to other people to maintain smooth relationships, but we can become tired due to the mental efforts required.

気 (*ki*, life energy, spirit, mind) in the expressions, 気をつかう (*ki o tsukau*, to be concerned with others) and 気をつける (*ki o tsukeru*, to pay attention), was introduced to Japan from China.

The Chinese language has many word combinations using 気. Japanese expressions, such as 元気 (*genki*, physical or mental vigor) and 気分 (*kibun*, feeling), came from Chinese words, but we use them with a different nuance. We formed a large number of expressions using 気. In fact, we have many using the character 気 alone, as seen below.

❀ 気をつける（注意力を働かせる）

　　Ki o tsukeru (*chuuiryoku o hatarakaseru*)

　　Attach the mind (to pay attention)

❀ 気をもむ（あれこれひどく心配する）

　　Ki o momu (*arekore hidoku shinpai suru*)

　　Crumble spirit (to worry terribly about random things)

❀ 気を配る（さまざまなところに配慮を加える）

　　Ki o kubaru (*samazama na tokoro ni hairyo o kuwaeru*)

　　Allocate mental energy (to parcel the weight of consideration to various factors)

❀ 気を回す（必要以上に考え、想像する）

Ki o mawasu（hitsuyou ijou ni kangae, souzou suru）

Spin one's mind (to overthink the situation and dream up scenarios)

❀ 気に病む（心にとめてあれこれ悩む）

Ki ni yamu（kokoro ni tomete arekore nayamu）

Mental sprit become sick (to obsess over one issue and worry about multiple outcomes)

❀ 気が置けない（気をつかう必要がない）

Ki ga okenai（ki o tsukau hitsuyou ga nai）

Not place the mind (not to worry about a person because he knows the situation)

気 indicates the function of the Japanese spirit. All the expressions above indicate our concern with others and our attention to the surroundings.

人並み *Hitonami,* Average or Like Others

Although nobody wants to be embarrassed in public, Japanese people especially fear sticking out in a group and being humiliated (*haji o kaku*) [see Chapter 2-2]. We are loath to speak out at meetings. We try to avoid speaking up first, without having an idea what others would say, because we are afraid of holding a different opinion than from the rest. For that reason, we tend to be cautious of what we say and do to avoid attracting unnecessary attention. Now, if we were put on the spot and asked to give an opinion, we could state みなさんと同じです (*minasan to onaji desu*, the same as others).

Japanese are fond of using the term 人並み (*hitonami*, ordinary). It literally means that a person is aligned at the same level as others in the group. We use it in the following expressions: 人並みの生活 (***hitonami*** *no seikatsu*, ordinary life), 人並みの暮らし (***hitonami*** *no kurashi*, ordinary living situation), 人並みの給料 (***hitonami*** *no kyuuryou*, average salary), and 人並みの能力 (***hitonami*** *no nouryoku*, average ability).

Example 1

お金持ちにならなくても、人並みの生活ができれば十分です。

Okanemochi ni naranakute mo, ***hitonami*** *no seikatsu ga dekireba juubun desu.*

Though I won't be rich, I'll be satisfied with a regular life.

Example 2

人並みの**給料**さえもらえれば、**出世**しなくてもいい。

Hitonami *no kyuuryou sae moraereba, shusse shinakute mo ii.*

If I can just earn a regular salary, I won't worry about becoming rich and famous.

When we ask Japanese children what they want to become, some might say, "I want to be a baseball player," or "I want to be a company president." However, if we put the same question to adults, many would reply that they would be content with an ordinary life.

Furthermore, we would likely say that we have average abilities, even though we may excel in some areas.

Example 3

A **英語**、お**上手**なんでしょう？

Eigo, ojouzu nan deshou?

You speak very good English, don't you?

B いやいや、まあ、**人並**みですよ。

Iyaiya, maa, hitonami desu yo.

Not really. My level is only average.

It is possible B in Example 3 is only being modest, but most Japanese people consciously try not to stand out. If we are better skilled, richer, or more prestigious than others around us, they might envy or resent us. Likewise, we would not want to be lower in prestige than others, so it is preferable to appear in the average range.

Recently, due to globalism, the Internet, and social networking, we have more opportunities to speak our mind. So, the appeal of the average and ordinary is gradually changing.

Normally, Japanese people go through life trying not to stand out in society. As we see in the following proverbs, we believe that we will be shunned if we stand out too much.

❁ 出る杭は打たれる

Deru kui wa utareru

The nail that sticks out gets hammered down.

❁ 高木は風に折らる

Kouboku wa kaze ni oraru

The towering tree will be snapped by the wind.

The concept of 人並みが一番 (*hitonami ga ichiban*, ordinary is best) comes from the Japanese understanding that to live in harmony with others, we must pay close attention to them to fit in with the group.

空気を読む　*Kuuki o Yomu,* To Read the Situation

Around 2007, the concept of "KY" became trendy in Japan. K is short for 空気 (*kuuki,* air) and Y is for 読めない (*yomenai,* cannot read). KY な人 (*kei wai na hito,* KY person) indicates 空気が読めない人 (*kuuki ga yomenai hito,* a person who cannot read the air, a person who cannot read the vibe of the room). 空気 (*kuuki,* air) represents the atmosphere of the situation or people. In this case, 読む (*yomu,* to read) is a combination of 考える (*kangaeru,* to think) and 推測する (*suisoku suru,* to guess). Hence, 空気を読む (*kuuki o yomu*) means to act fittingly with the feelings of the people present.

We even hear children saying あの子、KY だよね (*ano ko, kei wai dayo ne,* that kid is KY, he doesn't know what's going on) as a taunt. So, even from a young age, we expect each other to read people's feelings.

Example 1

この忙しい時期に自分だけ休みたいなんて、ちょっとは空気を読めよ。

*Kono isogashii jiki ni jibun dake yasumi tai nante, chotto wa **kuuki o yome** yo.*

You're asking for a day off when everybody is super busy? Can't you see the situation we're in?

Example 2

A 失恋した田中さんの前で、鈴木さんが恋人の自慢話ばかりするから、困っちゃった。

Shitsuren shita Tanaka-san no mae de, Suzuki-san ga koibito no jiman banashi bakari suru kara, komacchatta.

Miss Suzuki kept bragging about her boyfriend right in front of Miss Tanaka, who just went through a bad breakup. I didn't know what to do.

B 鈴木さんって、ほんと空気読めないね。

*Suzuki-san tte, honto **kuuki yomenai** ne.*

Miss Suzuki is completely clueless, right?

In Japan, we do not tend to speak up, so foreigners can be puzzled because they cannot discern what we are really thinking. However, we have the habit of feeling out situations and guessing other people's thoughts. This is called 暗黙の了解（***anmoku no ryoukai***, understanding in dark silence, tacit understanding）.

We also use similar expressions such as 以心伝心（***ishin denshin***, direct communication from master's heart to disciple's heart, good communication without speech）and 言わぬが花（***iwanu ga hana***, not speaking is a flower, some things are better left unsaid）. As you see, Japanese people treasure the quality of implicit understanding.

On the other hand, 口は災いの元（***kuchi wa wazawai no moto***, the mouth is the source of disaster, out of the mouth comes evil）is a proverb that teaches us to pay attention to what we say. It indicates that one careless word can cause deep problems, so we need to be vigilant.

Consequently, if we are surrounded by people that we hardly know or we cannot read the situation, it is better to play it safe in Japan. We normally sit back quietly or follow the actions of the others [see Chapter 3-3].

A deeper look

The proverb 目は口ほどにものを言う (*me wa kuchi hodo ni mono o iu*, the eyes speak better than the mouth) tells us that eyes of the speaker hold the true meaning.

Japanese people prefer communicating thoughts through attitude, facial expression, and subtext over plain speech. We call this ほのめかす (*honomekasu*, to imply) [see Chapter 5-2]. We feel delight when our intentions and feelings are conveyed without plain speech. For us, it means that the other person understands us well. To that purpose, he must have a keen eye for observation.

読む (*yomu*, to read) also holds the meaning of predicting something from observation. For example, we say 来年の世界の経済動向を読む (*rainen no sekai no keizai doukou o yomu*, predict the world economic trends over the next year).

The expression 相手の腹を読む (*aite no hara o yomu*, read the other's mind) is similar to *kuuki o yomu*. In this case, 腹 (*hara*, belly) indicates the other's true intentions.

We have other expressions using 腹 (*hara*) in daily life.

❀ 相手の腹がわからない (***aite no hara ga wakaranai***, to have no clue what the other is thinking)

❀ 腹を決める (***hara o kimeru***, to make up one's mind)

❀ 腹の探り合い (***hara no saguriai***, probing each other's true intention)

❀ 腹にもないことを言う (***hara ni mo nai koto o iu***, to say something we do not mean, to tell a white lie)

We also say そのことは腹にしまっておけ (*sono koto wa hara ni shimatte oke,* hold that thought in). It shows that Japanese people prefer to keep their opinions to themselves.

You can see that the ability to perceive and interpret the reality of a situation is considered a vital skill in Japanese society.

Everyday Conversations 2: The Real Intentions

考えておきます (*kangaete oki masu,* I'll think about it)

Conversation in a Japanese language class:

外国人学生： 先生、今度、みんなで花見に行きませんか？
Gaikokujin gakusei: Sensei, kondo, minna de hanami ni iki masen ka?
Foreign student: Professor, why don't we go to *hanami* (a cherry blossom viewing party) together?

日本語の先生： 花見？ いつ？
Nihongo no sensei: Hanami? Itsu?
Japanese teacher: Hanami? When?

外国人学生： 今度の日曜日です。上野公園の桜が満開だそうです。
Gaikokujin gakusei: Kondo no nichiyoubi desu. Ueno kouen no sakura ga mankai da sou desu.
Foreign student: Next Sunday. It looks like they will be at full bloom in Ueno Park.

日本語の先生： 今度の日曜日かぁ、考えておくよ。
Nihongo no sensei: Kondo no nichiyoubi kaa, kangaete oku yo.
Japanese teacher: Hmm, next Sunday... I will think about it.

外国人学生： じゃ、楽しみにしています。
Gaikokujin gakusei: Ja, tanoshimi ni shite i masu.
Foreign student: Well, then. I am looking forward to it.

Would you think this teacher will be going to the *hanami* party with his students? Foreign students would likely think that he will, because the teacher said he would think about it. However, most Japanese people would understand that he will not show up. Why is that?

We believe that we would hurt the feeling of the person with a direct refusal of the invitation. So, we might first say "I'll think about it," and then follow up a little later with, "I'm sorry but I can't make it this time." When you hear a Japanese person saying, "I'll think about it," you need to pay attention to his real intention.

The first meeting between a Japanese person and a foreigner:

外国人： 初めまして、どうぞよろしく。
Gaikokujin: *Hajime mashite, douzo yoroshiku.*
Foreigner: How do you do. Nice to meet you.

日本人： こちらこそ、よろしく。
Nihonjin: *Kochira koso, yoroshiku.*
Japanese: You, too. It's a pleasure.

外国人： あなたはどこに住んでいますか？
Gaikokujin: *Anata wa doko ni sunde i masu ka?*
Foreigner: Where do you live?

日本人： 東京の世田谷区です。
Nihonjin: *Toukyou no setagaya ku desu.*
Japanese: I live in Setagaya-ward, Tokyo.

外国人： いいところにお住まいですね。
Gaikokujin: *Ii tokoro ni osumai desu ne.*
Foreigner: That's a nice area to live in.

日本人： ええ、まあ。今度、一度遊びにきてください。
Nihonjin: *Ee, maa. Kondo, ichido asobi ni kite kudasai.*
Japanese: Well, not bad. Please come to my house sometime.

外国人： ありがとうございます。では、いつにしましょうか？
Gaikokujin: Arigatou gozaimasu. Dewa, itsu ni shi mashou ka?
Foreigner: Thank you very much. So, when would be a good time for you?

The Japanese person in the above conversation is now in trouble. For Japanese people, 一度遊びにきてください (*ichido asobi ni kite kudasai,* please come to my house sometime) is a simple greeting phrase to show our friendly intentions, but foreigners might think that the lip service is disingenuous. However, we believe it is discourteous not to invite a person when the conversation subject is our home. When we say 一度 (*ichido,* one time [in the future]), it really means, if we have a chance. It is meant to be understood that it is not a sure thing.

一度いっしょに飲みましょう (*ichido issho ni nomi mashou,* Let's go out for drinks sometime) also indicates that the meeting is in the uncertain future. In that case, a good response would be, ええ、今度また (*ee, kondo mata,* sure, sometime). If that person really wants to go out for drinks, he will ask you when would be a convenient day and time to meet.

Chapter 4

人間関係を大切にする
<small>にんげんかんけいたいせつ</small>

Ningen Kankei o Taisetsu ni Suru

To Value Relarionships

つきあい *Tsukiai*, Obligatory Companionship

4-1

つきあい (***tsukiai***, companionship) comes from the verb つきあう (*tsukiau*, to keep company with someone).

つきあう (*tsukiau*) originally meant 交際する (*kousai suru*, associate with someone on an individual basis/date someone). Later, it also took on the meaning of accompanying a person and doing things for his convenience (rather than one's own).

Example 1

山田君は十年近く**つきあった**彼女と、最近別れたそうだ。
*Yamada-kun wa juunen chikaku **tsukiatta** kanojo to, saikin wakareta sou da.*
I heard Mr. Yamada recently broke up with his girlfriend of almost ten years.

Example 2

疲れていたので早く帰りたかったが、先輩に**つきあって**飲みに行った。
*Tsukarete ita node hayaku kaeri takatta ga, senpai ni **tsukiatte** nomi ni itta.*
Though I was tired and wanted to go home early, I accompanied my senior for drinks.

Tsukiau in Example 1 simply states that he had a relationship with someone, but in Example 2, it indicates that the person was tied by social obligation to accompany his senior [see Chapter 7-4]. Here, the action of accompanying a person of higher rank to maintain a good relationship is called おつきあい (*otsukiai*, obligatory companionship).

Example 3

父は取引先との**おつきあい**で、毎週末ゴルフに行っている。

*Chichi wa torihikisaki to no **otsukiai** de, maishuumatsu gorufu ni itte iru.*

My father goes golfing every weekend to attend to his business client.

Example 4

あいつは**つきあい**が悪いから、もう誘うのはやめよう。

*Aitsu wa **tsukiai** ga warui kara, mou sasou no wa yameyou.*

That guy is unsociable; let's just stop inviting him.

Japanese people usually decide whether to participate in a friend's gathering or a business dinner, based on their relationship with the others involved. We do not tend to put as much importance on our own desires. We might think, "I refused last time, so I have to go this time," or "It will be difficult, but since my seniors are going, I'd better go with them."

If our schedule is extremely tight, we can say 顔だけ出します (*kao dake dashi masu*, I will present my face only, I will pop in). It means that we will leave shortly after appearing. Some might think it would be better not to go, if we would be leaving right away. Still, we know that our participation will be checked, and the difference between a brief appearance and a complete no-show is serious.

If we were to refuse invitations too often, we could be categorized as つきあいが悪い人 (*tsukiai ga warui hito*, an unsociable person). In Japanese society, which values good relationships, being marked as unsociable could be a great disadvantage. So, we must be prudent when we decline invitations.

When office workers go out drinking after work with their superiors or colleagues, it is called 飲みニケーション (*nominikeeshon*/*nomi*-nication, communication over drinks). This word is formed from two words: 飲む (*nomu*,

61

to drink) and communication. We think that when we drink together, we can keep our relationships smooth in an informal and relaxed setting. The term had gone out of vogue, but reemerged recently, drawing attention to the issues of stress and communication in the workplace.

愛想 *Aiso*, Amiability

愛想（*aiso/aisou*, amiability）is a cultivated attitude, which serves to give a good impression to others. In particular, it relates to the proper manner of greeting people, including choice of language and facial expressions. People in the service industry must show impeccable *aiso*, but we also apply it to daily life.

Example 1

この店の店員は、みんなニコニコしていて愛想がいい。

*Kono mise no ten'in wa, minna nikoniko shite ite **aiso ga ii**.*

The salesclerks in this shop are all smiles and eager to please.

Example 2

鈴木先輩はいつも無愛想だから、声をかけづらい。

*Suzuki-senpai wa itsumo **buaisou** da kara, koe o kake zurai.*

Our senior, Mr. Suzuki, is always sullen and unsociable, so he's hard to approach.

In Example 1, 愛想がいい（人）(*aiso ga ii* [*hito*], amiable [person]) is a person whose expression and attitude are friendly and approachable, and ニコニコ (*nikoniko*) indicates a smiley face. However, in Example 2, a person who does not respond well to greetings or questions and presents a stolid face is 愛想が悪い (*aiso ga warui*, amiability is bad, unfriendly), 愛想がない (*aiso ga nai*, no amiability, unfriendly) or 無愛想だ (*buaisou da*, not friendly).

If 愛想がいい (*aiso ga ii*, amiable) is insincere, it can be employed as irony.

Example 3
彼女は**愛想**がいいばかりで、肝心なときには助けてくれない。

*Kanojo wa **aiso ga ii** bakari de, kanjin na toki ni wa tasukete kurenai.*

She is always super friendly, but never helps when I need it.

Amiable is better than unamiable, but if it is ingenuine, it takes on a rather bad meaning. For that, we use the term, 愛想笑い (***aiso warai***, fake smile). If a person forces smiles or laughter to hold onto an important relationship, that would be ***aiso warai***.

Example 4
課長は部長の機嫌をうかがって、いつも**愛想笑い**をしている。

*Kachou wa buchou no kigen o ukagatte, itsumo **aiso warai** o shite iru.*

The section chief always checks the chief director, and gives him a fake smile.

We use 愛想 (*aiso*) in different ways.

Example 5
何度も借金を頼まれて、彼には**愛想**がつきた。

*Nando mo shakkin o tanomarete, kare ni wa **aiso ga tsukita**.*

He kept asking me to lend him money, so I finally got fed up.

愛想がつきる (***aiso ga tsukiru***, to run out of smiles) and 愛想をつかす *aiso o tsukasu*, to use up all smiles) are used to describe a change of perception with someone. We had a good feeling at first, but we gave up due to his behavior.

愛嬌 (***aikyou***, attractiveness) is similar to 愛想 (*aiso*). It is commonly used to describe the cute gestures and facial expressions by children and women. We say この子は愛嬌がない (*kono ko wa aikyou ga nai*, this child does not act cute) or 彼女は美人ではないが愛嬌のある顔をしている (*kanojo wa bijin de wa nai ga aikyou no aru kao o shite iru*, she is not beautiful, but has a sweet face).

In Japanese society, it is best to communicate with an amiable attitude, but without faking it.

A deeper look

There is an odd usage of the term, お愛想 (*oaiso*, the tallied bill requested by the customer at a traditional Japanese restaurant).

Although customers say, お愛想をお願いします (*oaiso o onegai shi masu*, please let us pay), we must note that it is an improper use of term. Logically, お愛想 (*oaiso*, the check) should come from the restaurant that offers *aiso* (friendliness), not stated by the customer that receives *aiso*. According to one theory, restaurants started to use it because they felt sorry to make their customers pay. Some say that giving the check to the customer is the final service done by a restaurant, so we use this term. In truth, its origin is unknown.

礼儀 *Reigi*, Manners and Etiquette

In Japanese society, we place the importance of 礼儀 (*reigi*, manners and etiquette), up with 義理 (*giri*, obligation) [see Chapter 7-4] and 遠慮 (*enryo*, restraint) [see Chapter 3-1].

Reigi refers to the actions taken to show respect to others. In Japan, the application of etiquette differs widely, depending on age, social status, and the association with *uchi* and *soto* [see Chapter 1-1]. Due to the sincere nature of Japanese people, and our long history with the warring class system, we have developed complex rules around *reigi*.

Examples of *reigi* include daily greetings, the use of the proper language for different situations, and the gesture of bowing. If we do not follow the criteria of etiquette, we can be considered 礼儀知らず (***reigi shirazu***, not knowing etiquette, rude).

Example 1

隣の家のご主人はしつけが厳しいので、子どもたちはみな礼儀正しい。

*Tonari no ie no goshujin wa shitsuke ga kibishii node, kodomotachi wa mina **reigi tadashii**.*

Our neighbor's husband is a strict disciplinarian, so his children are all well-mannered [see Chapter 1-3].

Example 2

新人なのに先輩にあいさつもしないで帰るなんて、なんて礼儀知らずなやつだ。

*Shinjin na noni senpai ni aisatsu mo shinaide kaeru nante, nante **reigi shirazu** na yatsu da.*
The newbie just upped and left, without a nod to his seniors. What a rube!

Japanese people value manners in daily life and are quite sensitive to rude behavior. For that reason, parents and teachers are stringent in teaching children to use proper greetings.

For instance, we almost always say 失礼します (*shitsurei shimasu*, I am doing a rude thing, excuse me) when entering another's space and leaving from it. We would also say it when leaving the workplace ahead of our superiors and colleagues. Some might think it is a rote expression of greeting or excusing oneself, but we believe it would be discourteous not to say it. Even in a close relationship, we could lend an impression of disrespect if we do not use the expression.

In their first orientation, Japanese companies strictly educate new employees to use appropriate greetings. Even part-timers must take training sessions to learn how to greet customers properly.

Greetings are crucial at all levels of Japanese society. ***Reigi*** includes polite language, gestures, attitudes, and manners, but greeting people is the most essential and basic component [see Everyday Conversation 1].

A deeper look

We learn 礼に始まり、礼に終わる (*rei ni hajimari, rei ni owaru*, start with a bow and end with a bow) in the world of Japanese traditional sports such as *kendo*, *judo*, and *karate*. Similarly, in normal society, we solemnly value *reigi*.

Still, there are some gatherings where we may let go of *reigi*, called 無礼講 (*bureikou*, uncermonious meeting, informal party). 無礼 (*burei*, no courtesy) is a slightly more formal version of 失礼 (*shitsurei*, lose courtesy, rude).

今日の宴会は無礼講だ。遠慮なく飲んでくれ。
Kyou no enkai wa bureikou da. Enryo naku nonde kure.
Today's party isn't formal. Drink as much as you want.

The literal meaning is that we can drink freely and relinquish formal manners without consideration of our elders or superiors. In fact, this directive comes from our superiors, so they are just allowing us to relax a bit. We can never forego proper manners.

慇懃無礼 (*ingin burei*, hypocritical courtesy) describes an attitude, which is superficially polite, but rude in intent. If someone acts overpolite to a person but actually looks down on him, the attitude is called *ingin burei*. Because of this, we must be careful that our courtesy is sincere.

In Japan, we all used to live in *tatami* rooms. *Tatami* is a type of thick mat made with rice straws. The official way to sit on *tatami* was かしこまる (*kashikomaru*, to sit respectfully), also called 正座する (*seiza suru*, to sit properly, to sit upright with both knees folded).

In formal settings, such as wedding ceremonies and funerals, we used to sit in that manner, but we got tired after a while and our legs went numb. Even so, we had to remain in the posture until the host told us, どうぞ膝を崩してください (*douzo hiza o kuzushite kudasai*, please relax your knees) or お楽になさってください (*oraku ni nasatte kudasai*, please relax). Nowadays, we often can sit in chairs.

The verb かしこまる (*kashikomaru*) originally comes from かしこむ (*kashikomu*), which meant to fear and respect the other, so facing the other while sitting upright embodied *kashikomaru*. In a business setting, we use the term かしこまりました (**kashikomari mashita**, I accept your request or order with fear and respect) to mean "Certainly" or "It would be my pleasure."

本音と建前
Honne to Tatemae, True Feelings and Official Stance

Japanese people often suppress feelings or refrain from stating opinions until they assess the situation or the standpoint of others. Especially, in a business meeting, which should be the best venue to debate the ideas, we tend to offer an innocuous opinion that no one would oppose. We call an official opinion or a policy that would not offend anyone, 建前 (*tatemae*, façade, official stance).

The opposite term to that is 本音 (*honne*, true sound, true feelings or opinions). In the Japanese business scene, people can use both *honne* and *tatemae* to their benefit.

Example 1

A社が今度新しく始めるサービスは、建前では顧客のためと言っているが、実際は社内の事業改革が目的のようだ。

*A-sha ga kondo atarashiku hajimeru saabisu wa, **tatemae** de wa kokyaku no tame to itte iru ga, jissai wa shanai no jigyou kaikaku ga mokuteki no you da.*

Company A states that their new service is a benefit to customers, but, in reality, the purpose is to streamline their own business.

Example 2

会議に社長がいると、参加者はみんな建前ばかりで、なかなか本音を言わない。

*Kaigi ni shachou ga iru to, sankasha wa minna **tatemae** bakari de, nakanaka **honne** o iwanai.*

Whenever the president is in the meeting, everybody else just follows the group. They hardly ever speak their minds.

It is generally known that Japanese people do not actively participate in meetings, and, if we do, we would offer only the general opinion of the group. We strive to avoid conflict, because we treasure 和 (***wa***, peace, harmony of the group) above all else.

However, if we utter only *tatemae*, we may be criticized. あの人は建前ばかりで、いつまでたっても本音を言わない (*ano hito wa tatemae bakari de, itsumade tatte mo honne o iwanai*, that guy only repeats what everyone thinks; he never states his own opinions).

Additionally, if a person keeps changing his opinions based on the current drift, people will not trust him, using the expression, あの人は建前をすぐ崩す (*ano hito wa tatemae o sugu kuzusu*, that guy changes his opinions with the weather).

If people either offered only the standard opinions or they remained stuck on their own feelings, the discussion would never move forward. To ensure that meetings are harmonious and efficient, members might ask each other to voice their opinions beforehand. That way, they can weigh the general direction of ideas and adjust them, so that conflicts will not surface. We call this 根回し (**nemawashi**, digging round root, behind-the-scenes negotiation).

Honne and *tatemae* are also pervasive in daily life.

Example 3

A みんなケンカしないで、仲よくしないといけませんよ。

Minna kenka shinaide, nakayoku shinai to ike masen yo.

Everyone should get along without fighting.

B そりゃそうだけど、ひどい悪口を言われたものだから…

Sorya sou da kedo, hidoi waruguchi o iwareta mono da kara...

Maybe so, but I got seriously dissed...

In Example 3, A says *tatemae* and B says *honne*. Again, *tatemae* is the statement of principal that nobody can contest, and *honne* is the declaration of true opinion.

A deeper look

Most people have the ability to hide the true feelings behind their statements. Japanese people, in particular, have a reputation for holding in their *honne*. So when *honne* does come out, it is called 本音を吐く (***honne o haku***, to spit out one's true feeling, give oneself away) or 本音を漏らす (*honne o morasu*, to let out one's true feelings, bare the truth).

音 (*ne*, sound) of 本音 (*honne*, true feelings), here, is the voice of truth. We also say 音をあげる (***ne o ageru***, to emit voice of defeat, admit defeat) and ぐうの音も出ない (***guu no ne mo denai***, not even a choking voice comes out, struck dumb, utter defeat).

おかげさま *Okagesama*, Your Benevolence

We originally used the term おかげさま (*okagesama*, a respected person's good will) to thank God or Buddha at a temple or a shrine, to pray for assistance or good luck. Now, we also use the expression to thank people when we benefit from their help or support.

Example 1

先生　大学合格おめでとう！

Sensei　*Daigaku goukaku omedetou!*
Teacher　Congratulations on your college acceptance!

学生　ありがとうございます。先生のご指導の**おかげ**です。

Gakusei　*Arigatou gozai masu. Sensei no goshidou no **okage** desu.*
Student　Thank you very much. It is all thanks to your guidance.

When expressing deep gratitude to someone, it is better to say あなたの**おかげで** (*anata no **okage** de*, due to your help) rather than a simple ありがとう (*arigatou*, thank you). That person will be happy to hear that his assistance made a difference.

When we feel indebted to a person, it is important to express the feeling of appreciation skillfully. Japanese people value expressions of gratitude in daily life.

Example 2

A こんにちは。お元気そうですね。

Konnichiwa. Ogenki sou desu ne.

Hello. You're looking well.

B ええ、**おかげさまで**。

*Ee, **okagesama de**.*

Yes, thanks to you.

Example 3

A お母さんの具合はいかがですか。

Okaasan no guai wa ikaga desu ka.

How's your mother feeling?

B **おかげさまで**、もうすっかりよくなりました。

***Okagesama de**, mou sukkari yoku nari mashita.*

Thanks to your care, she has nearly recovered.

Example 2 shows how ***okagesama de*** is used as a basic greeting. In Example 3, however, we give the other party credit, even if they tangibly had nothing to do with helping the situation. We express our gratitude for their continued attention and kindness to us, not necessarily thanking them for specific acts of kindness.

A deeper look

Okage is principally used to express gratitude to someone, whose help and cooperation benefited us. However, we can also use it sarcastically to express disapproval of someone, when things turn out badly.

A君が道を間違えたおかげで、十分で着くところを一時間もドライブさせられちゃったよ。

A-kun ga michi o machigaeta okage de, juppun de tsuku tokoro o ichijikan mo doraibu saserare chatta yo.

Thanks to Mr. A taking a wrong turn, we ended up driving an hour—what should have been ten minutes.

Here, we normally would express blame by saying, A君のせいで (*A-kun no sei de*, bad result because of Mr. A), but instead, we say, A君のおかげで (*A-kun no okage de*, thanks to the graciousness [of his blunder]) as sarcasm to mock A.

Everyday Conversations 3: Showing Agreement or Comprehension

なるほど (*naruhodo*, I see)

Conversation between company colleagues:

佐藤： 鈴木さん、出張だったそうですね。
Satou: *Suzuki-san, shucchou datta sou desu ne.*
Mr. Suzuki, I heard you had a business trip.

鈴木： うん、今度の新商品の売り込みで、中国へ行っていたんだ。
Suzuki: *Un, kondo no shin shouhin no urikomi de, chuugoku e itte itan da.*
Right. I went to China to promote our new product.

佐藤： へえ、そうですか。で、どうですか、反応は…
Satou: *Hee, sou desu ka. De, dou desu ka, hannou wa...*
Is that right? So, how did it go?

鈴木： そうだね。なかなかいいよ。いま中国は景気がいいからね。
Suzuki: *Sou da ne. Nakanaka ii yo. Ima chuugoku wa keiki ga ii kara ne.*
Well, it went fairly well. The Chinese economy is good now.

佐藤： そうなんですか。じゃ、ずいぶん売れそうですね。
Satou: *Sou nan desu ka. Ja, zuibun ure sou desu ne.*
Really? So, it looks like it will sell.

鈴木： うん、それになんといっても、人口が多いからマーケットも大きい。
Suzuki: *Un, soreni nanto itte mo, jinkou ga ooi kara maaketto mo ookii.*
Right, and the large population offers a wide market.

佐藤： なるほど…
Satou: *Naruhodo...*
I see.

鈴木：　1%の人が買ってくれても、一千万個は売れる計算になる。

Suzuki: *Ippaasento hito ga katte kurete mo, issenmanko wa ureru keisan ni naru.*

If one percent of the population buys our product, we'll sell ten million units.

佐藤：　たしかに…

Satou: *Tashika ni...*

Surely...

Conversations are important in any country, but Japanese people make extra efforts to go along with the speaker. Listeners demonstrate that they are listening with facial expressions, gestures, and use certain expressions, such as *hee* (really?) or *naruhodo* (so, that's how it works; I see). The action is called 相づちを打つ (*aizuchi o utsu*, peppering the conversation with responses).

Aizuchi o utsu is a technique used by Japanese blacksmiths. By alternating in quick succession, two smiths strike the same piece of red-hot iron with their hammers. We use this expression to describe a conversation that goes back and forth with good rhythm.

Some might think Japanese people's habit of responding to each and every sentence is too much. But for us, the replies indicate that we are engaged in the story, and we wish to sustain a pleasant conversation.

Chapter 5

表現を抑える

Hyougen o Osaeru

To Restrain Personal Expressions

控えめ Hikaeme, Restrained or Moderate

The word 控えめ (*hikaeme*, restrained) is a combination of 控える (*hikaeru*, to hold back from doing something) with め (*me*), which describes a degree of amount, such as 少なめ (*sukuname*, slightly less), and 多め (*oome*, a little extra). We employ *hikaeru* to avoid extremes of behavior or actions.

Example 1

体の調子が悪いときは、お酒は控えめにしたほうがいいですよ。

Karada no choushi ga warui toki wa, osake wa hikaeme ni shita hou ga ii desu yo.

When you're under the weather, you'd better ease up on the liquor.

However, if a doctor tells you お酒は控えてください (*osake wa hikaete kudasai*, please cut back on the alcohol), it actually means 飲まないでください (*nomanaide kudasai*, do not drink it at all).

We can also see 塩分控えめ (*enbun hikaeme*, low sodium) or 油分控えめ (*aburabun hikaeme*, low fat) on food packaging to indicate that the food contains a lower than usual amount of a component.

So, when we use 控えめ (*hikaeme*) to describe a person, what does that mean?

Example 2

その選手は優勝したのに、言葉が**控えめ**で好感が持てる。

*Sono senshu wa yuushou shita noni, kotoba ga **hikaeme** de koukan ga moteru.*
We like that player. He uses humble words, even after taking the championship.

Japanese people do not favor a person who blurts out opinions and openly expresses feelings or desires. Adults should be able to hold in their emotions in respect to others or to the situation. We need to show humility, especially when we are successful or attain a higher status. 控えめな人 (***hikaeme** na hito*, a modest person) is a person who can control his emotions and remain calm.

つつましい (***tsutsumashii***, modest) is similar to 控えめ (***hikaeme***). It also refers to modesty and the ability to hold one's emotions in check. The word comes from an ancient word 慎む (*tsutsumu*; read as *tsutsushimu* in modern Japanese). 慎む (*tsutsushimu*) carries the meaning of 控える (*hikaeru*, to restrain oneself from acting), but adds the element of being careful to avoid mistakes. Therefore, when we describe a person as ***tsutsumashii*** instead of ***hikaeme***, it emphasizes that the person is attentive to others and cautious to avoid discourtesy [see Chapter 3-1].

Example 3

妻は、夫の後ろにつつましく控えている。

*Tsuma wa, otto no ushiro ni **tsutsumashiku** hikaete iru.*
The wife quietly stands behind her husband.

Example 3 portrays a wife who does not upstage and silently supports her husband. In the Japanese old tradition, women were supposed to protect men's honor at all times. Therefore, we use the adjective つつましい (*tsutsumashii*, modest) to describe a preference for women who are modest and quiet. However, we also praise men by saying 非常に謙虚でつつましい態度の人 (*hijou ni kenkyo de tsutsumashii taido no hito*, an extremely humble and modest person).

In general, Japanese people prefer modest attitudes and controlled emotions, so the terms **hikaeme** and **tsutsumashii** present a very positive image.

A deeper look

A person whose character is **hikaeme** would not meddle in a discussion, even if he has better knowledge of the field. On the other hand, if someone aggressively interferes in other people's business without being asked, that action is called 出過ぎる (*desugiru*, to obtrude). We can berate these people by saying,

出過ぎたまねをするな！
Desugita mane o suru na!
Don't butt in!

When a person makes comments or gives unneeded advice without having the specific knowledge or experience, we call that action でしゃばる (*deshabaru*, to be pushy) and the person is でしゃばり (*deshabari*, a busybody or meddler).

If a child interrupts an adult conversation, he would be scolded.

おまえはよくわかっていないんだから、でしゃばるんじゃない！
Omae wa yoku wakatte inain da kara, deshabarun ja nai!
You don't know what you're talking about. Stop butting in!

Being modest and restrained is a virtue, so *deshabari* is frowned upon in Japan.

しゃしゃりでる (***shashari deru***, to poke one's nose in) carries a much stronger image of rudeness to describe a pushy person. If a random guy showed up to a public venue and poked his nose in where it didn't belong, he could be sharply rebuked with:

おまえなんかしゃしゃりでる場ではない、引っ込んでいろ！
Omae nanka shashari deru ba de wa nai, hikkonde iro!
Dude! This is no place to butt in. Take a hike!

ほのめかす *Honomekasu,* To Give a Hint or Imply

Foreign people often consider Japanese people to be 曖昧 (*aimai*, ambiguous) and 何を考えているか、よくわからない (*nani o kangaete iru ka, yoku wakaranai*, we can't tell what they're thinking). We usually refrain from openly expressing our feelings and hold our opinions back in respect to others, which can give that impression.

However, in Japan, we believe that people should be able to read each other's true feelings from non-verbal cues or subtext. We have proverbs such as 以心伝心 (*ishin denshin*, what the mind thinks, the heart transmits; heart-to-heart communication) and 目は口ほどにものを言う (*me wa kuchi hodo ni mono o iu*, the eyes speak as well as the mouth, the eyes are the window to the soul).

The term ほのめかす (*honomekasu*, to give a hint or imply) indicates the use of subtext and demeanor to convey our true thoughts. Generally, Japanese people can infer the true meaning by reading the cues.

In Japan, we prefer this form of communication over an open discussion of issues. In fact, we may lose respect if a person speaks too plainly. We describe that as あからさま (*akarasama*, too open, too straight). Japanese people prefer modesty and restraint [see Chapter 5-1], so that attitude is disparaged.

Example 1

上司から、職場の異動を**ほのめかされた**。

Joushi kara, shokuba no idou o ***honomekasareta****.*

My boss implied that I may be shuffled to another branch.

Example 2

彼女は彼と目が合うと、**あからさまに**視線をそらした。

*Kanojo wa kare to me ga au to, **akarasama ni** shisen o sorashita.*

After locking eyes with him, she visibly averted her gaze.

The word あからさま (*akarasama*, open, straightforward) is made of 明るい (*akarui*, bright) and さま (*sama*, appearance). In our society, we consider the forthright display of emotions and opinions to be rude and lacking class. So, *akarasama* holds a negative meaning about revealing something outwardly. In Example 2, the woman displayed her dislike of the man with her overt reaction.

Different cultures have different taboos. In Japan, it is taboo to talk openly about money, sex, or naked desires.

While ほのめかす (*honomekasu*) is the action of hinting at something below the surface, a person who exemplifies a quality without making a big deal out of it is described as さりげない (***sarigenai***, nonchalant).

Example 3

彼女の**さりげない**おしゃれには、好感が持てる。

*Kanojo no **sarigenai** oshare ni wa, koukan ga moteru.*

We like her veiled fashion statement.

Example 4

課長は**さりげなく**部下に注意を与えた。

*Kachou wa **sarigenaku** buka ni chuui o ataeta.*

The section chief gave a quiet warning to his subordinate.

さりげない (*sarigenai*) indicates that something is not readily apparent, or it does not appear in the usual manner. In this way, it shows that the appearance or act is obscure. In Example 1, her fashion, though not obvious and flashy, is natural and chic. Example 2 demonstrates the thoughtfulness of the section chief, who deftly communicated a warning without attracting attention from the other employees.

Japanese people often communicate without speaking. Therefore, we must be careful not to miss signals from facial expressions, body language, and gestures.

A deeper look

We also use euphemisms to avoid saying things outright.

Example 1

あの人忙しそうだから、私たち、今日行くのは遠慮したほうがいいかもしれないね。

Ano hito isogashisou da kara, watashitachi, kyou iku no wa enryo shita hou ga ii kamo shirenai ne.

He seems kind of busy, so maybe better not to visit him at home today.

In Example 1, the speaker substitutes 遠慮する (*enryo suru*, to refrain from doing something for his sake) [see Chapter 3-1] for 行かない (*ikanai*, not to go), which is the true meaning.

これみよがし (***koremiyogashi***, ostentatious, exaggerated) is a phrase from old Japanese, which originally meant これを見てほしい (*kore o mite hoshii*, I want people to see this). It is now condensed to a single word, which holds the negative connotation of ostentatious or flagrant. It can be used to describe a person driving an arrogant point home with an exaggerated display of actions and attitude, rather than words.

Example 2

彼は**これみよがし**にお金を投げて渡した。

*Kare wa **koremiyogashi** ni okane o nagete watashita.*

He threw the money at her to make a point.

In Example 2, by throwing the money at her, he demonstrates his contempt.

Likewise, あてつけ（***atetsuke***, insinuation）is a way to convey a bad message through innuendo or a spiteful action.

Example 3

A 妹さん、料理が上手だね。

Imoutosan, ryouri ga jouzu da ne.

Your little sister cooks well, doesn't she?

B 何？ それって私への**あてつけ**？

*Nani? Sorette watashi e no **atetsuke**?*

Say what? Is that really a dig at me?

In Example 3, B is angry, because she thinks A is criticizing her own cooking by praising her sister's skills.

角を立てない *Kado o Tatenai,* Avoid Offense

角 (*kado*, corner) is a sharp and pointed aspect of something. If it touches a person, it will hurt. We say 角を立てる (*kado o tateru*, to push an issue that creates hard feelings) when we hurt another person's feelings with words.

Example 1

A 私とつきあってください。

Watashi to tsukiatte kudasai.

Please be my girlfriend.

B 私はあなたが嫌いです。

Watashi wa anata ga kirai desu.

I just don't like you.

B's straight response will hurt A or make him angry. Some might think it is better to speak candidly, but others believe that is 角が立つ (*kado ga tatsu,* sharp point stands up, it is too direct and hurtful). We must be careful to avoid hard feelings, if we want to keep good relationships. The application of that is 角を立てない (*kado o tatenai,* avoid offense).

Usually, Japanese people will communicate in a nicer way to smooth things over. For example, instead of B's response, she could have said, もう別に恋人がいます (*mou betsu ni koibito ga imasu,* I have a boyfriend already) or 今は仕事に夢中なので (*ima wa shigoto ni muchuu na node,* I am immersed in my work now) to let him down nicely. It is considered acceptable to tell a white lie to make the other person feel better. He would likely know it is a lie, but accepts it with the knowledge that she cares enough to maintain harmony [see Chapter 3-2]. Another example would be to say 味があるねえ (*aji ga aru nee*, it has taste) when we have to comment on a bad drawing.

ものは言いようで角が立つ (***mono wa iiyou de kado ga tatsu***, the way we speak can cause harm) is a proverb. We must choose our language carefully, because words can hurt or anger people.

Example 2

A ここ、間違えないように注意してね。

Koko, machigaenai you ni chuui shite ne.

Be careful not to make a mistake right here.

B わかってるよ、それぐらい。

Wakatteru yo, sore gurai.

Ok, I know that much already.

A だって、いつも間違えるじゃない！

Datte, itsumo machigaeru ja nai!

Yeah, but you keep flubbing it!

We might hear this kind of conversation among friends or coworkers. A is trying to support B with advice, but B's response is 角のある (***kado no aru***, has a sharp corner, hurtful), which angers A. If B simply replied with a "thank you," he would not risk harming the relationship.

We must be careful when selecting words. Among friends, it might not be such a big deal, but, if we misspeak in an official capacity, we could lose clients or get fired.

A deeper look

During the Asuka period (592–710), 聖徳太子 (*Shoutoku Taishi*, Prince Shotoku) propagated Buddhism in Japan. 和をもって貴しとなす (***wa o motte toutoshi to nasu***, harmony is to be valued) is one of his sayings, still referred to in Japan. It speaks to the extreme importance of maintaining harmonious relationships with others. The terms 角を立てない (***kado o tatenai***) and 丸くおさめる (*maruku osameru*, rounding things out to deal with complaints) support that wisdom.

We also must be careful to 空気を読む (*kuuki o yomu*, to read the room) [see Chapter 3-4] and ほのめかす (*honomekasu*, to use nonverbal language) [see Chapter 5-2].

Everyday Conversations 4: Softening the Impact

ちょっと (*chotto*, a little)

A chat between friends in a clothing store:

春子： 夏子、この服どう？　似合う？

Haruko: *Natsuko, kono fuku dou? Niau?*

Natsuko, what do you think of this dress? Does it look good on me?

夏子： うーん、ちょっと…。なんとなくサイズが合っていないような…。

Natsuko: *Uun, **chotto**... **Nantonaku** saizu ga atte inai **you na**...*

Well, I'm not quite sure... Somehow, the size doesn't seem right.

春子： そう？　…じゃあ、こっちのは？

Haruko: *Sou? ... Jaa, kocchi no wa?*

Oh, really? Then, how about this one?

夏子： うーん、たぶん、もうちょっと薄い色のほうがいいかも…。

Natsuko: *Uun, **tabun**, mou chotto usui iro no hou ga **ii kamo**...*

Hmm, maybe a slightly lighter color would be better...

春子： そうかぁ。じゃあ、買うのやめようかなぁ。

Haruko: *Sou kaa. Jaa, kau no yameyou kanaa.*

You think so? Well, maybe I shouldn't buy one now.

Japanese people commonly use equivocal expressions such as ちょっと (*chotto*, a little), なんとなく (*nantonaku*, somehow) and たぶん (*tabun*, maybe), or we sometimes will not finish the sentence, which could imply other things [see Chapter 5-2]. That could partially explain why some foreigners see us as ambiguous and hard to read. Be that as it may, our use of vague language stems from our efforts to be considerate of others. We do not wish to make other people hurt or uncomfortable by uttering strong opinions, or by rebuffing their opinions [see Chapter 3-1]. Expressions such as *chotto* and *tabun* can soften the impact of our opinions or statements on others.

When we speak to a superior or a client, we must pay special attention to what we say [see Chapter 3-2]. Below are some phrases we might use.

❀ ひとつお願いがあるんですが…

Hitotsu onegai ga arun desu ga...

I have one small favor to ask you...

(*Hitotsu* makes the favor seem easier to swallow.)

❀ **A** 僕は行くけど、君はどうする？

Boku wa iku kedo, kimi wa dou suru?

I'm going, but how about you?

B 私はちょっと…

Watashi wa **chotto**...

I am a little...

(Saying *chotto* and trailing off indicates a softened form of refusal.)

❀ 私はともかく、彼がいやがるでしょう。

Watashi wa **tomokaku**, *kare ga iyagaru deshou.*

Putting my feelings aside, I'm pretty sure he won't like it.

(Using *tomokaku* to avoid saying one's true feelings.)

❀ これは犯罪と言ってもいいのではないか。

Kore wa hanzai to **itte mo ii no de wa nai ka**.

You could say that it is a crime.

(*Itte mo ii no de wa nai ka* softens an assertion or avoids an outright claim.)

As you can see, Japanese people use numerous expressions to soften the impact of a message. Indeed, softening language, such as *chotto* and *tabun*, is often employed unconsciously, but it figures prominently in general speech. We can even hear it in formal debate, where rendering opinions and criticizing the opponent's view is expected. We wish to avoid creating hard feelings and possible problems in the future. Principally, we always strive to be sensitive to the people around us.

Chapter 6

精神主義を好む

Seishinshugi o Konomu
To Embrace Spiritualism

がんばる Ganbaru, To Endeavor

6-1

After World War II, Japan became one of the top countries to bounce back economically, despite its small land size and limited resources. That growth is a tribute to the diligence and dedicated work ethic of the Japanese people. That spirit is exemplified by the prominent use of the verb がんばる (*ganbaru*, to tough it out) in daily life.

Example 1

高校生になったら、勉強もスポーツもがんばります。

*Koukousei ni nattara, benkyou mo supootsu mo **ganbari masu**.*

When I begin high school, I will work hard at my studies and in sports.

Example 2

上司　今月の売上目標、月末までに達成できるのか？

Joushi　Kongetsu no uriage mokuhyou, getsumatsu made ni tassei dekiru no ka?

Superior　Can you reach the sales target by the end of the month?

部下　はい。達成できるよう、**がんばります**！

*Buka　Hai. Tassei dekiru you, **ganbari masu**!*

Subordinate　Yes. I will pull out all stops to get there!

In Example 2, even if the subordinate is not sure he can achieve the sales target, he declares *ganbari masu* instead of できません (*deki masen*, he cannot do it) to display his positive attitude.

In Japan, we use *ganbaru* to declare our resolve. A student might say, いい成績がとれるように、がんばります (*ii seiseki ga toreru you ni, ganbari masu*, I will work hard to get good grades), an office worker might say, 目標達成のために、がんばります (*mokuhyou tassei no tame ni, ganbari masu*, I will do my best to reach the goal), and a politician might say, 国民のために、がんばります (*kokumin no tame ni, ganbari masu*, I will commit fully to the people of this country).

We also use がんばって or がんばれ (*ganbatte* or *ganbare*, go for it!) to encourage and cheer on an individual or a group.

Example 3

優勝目指して、**がんばってください**！
Yuushou mezashite, ***ganbatte kudasai****!*
Give it your all, and bring home the championship!

Example 4

A 今晩、ついに彼女にプロポーズすることにしたよ。
Konban, tsuini kanojo ni puropoozu suru koto ni shita yo.
I finally made up my mind to propose to her tonight.

B そうか、**がんばれ**よ！
Souka, ***ganbare*** *yo!*
Wow, really? Good luck, man!

In Japan, we often exchange the set phrases, がんばって or がんばれ (*ganbatte or ganbare*, do your best!) and がんばります (*ganbari masu*, I will. Thanks for the encouragement).

The essence of *ganbaru* is to keep going, even when it is difficult to attain the goal. So, if you were to say, "*ganbare*!" to someone already working at maximum capacity, you might imply that he is not working hard enough. 無理する (*muri suru*, to do the impossible, to work too hard) is similar to *ganbaru*, but here, it means to push beyond one's limits of ability or stamina [see Chapter 6-3]. Since it would be cruel to say *ganbare* to someone who is already doing more than enough, we could say 無理しないでね (*muri shinaide ne*, don't overdo it) instead. A good reply to this kind of encouragement would be 無理してでも、がんばります (*muri shite demo, ganbari masu*, though it is too much, I will stick with it).

In Ruth Benedict's *The Chrysanthemum and the Sword*, she noted that Japan tried to win World War II by pitting spiritual strength against America's material power. She posits that it is an intrinsic principle of Japanese nature. Even now, Japanese people favor this spirit, and we readily say がんばります (*ganbari masu*, I'll keep trying) or 努力します (*doryoku shi masu*, I will make efforts) whenever facing challenges or hardships.

During a period of high economic growth in the 1960s, Japanese workers were nicknamed, 働き蜂 (*hataraki bachi*, worker bees) or 企業戦士 (*kigyou senshi*, corporate warriors) because of their staunch work ethic. Regrettably, this do-or-die spirit took a heavy toll. The high rates of work-related depression and 過労死 (*karoushi*, death by overwork) were severe, finally receiving due attention with worker protections in the new millennium. Japanese companies, now obliged to protect their employees, forbade excess overtime and increased vacation time. Nevertheless, the Japanese work ethic persists, and the thought of resting while others work engenders guilt. So, it is true that many still balk at taking days off, even with the encouragement of their company.

The following proverbs speak to the Japanese spirit of diligence.

❀ 精神一到何事か成らざらん

Seishin ittou nanigoto ka narazaran.

With a focused mind, there's nothing you cannot do. Where there's a will, there's a way.

❀ 為せば成る　為さねば成らぬ　何事も

Naseba naru nasaneba naranu nanigoto mo.

Do, and it will be done; don't do, and it will never be done; that applies to all things.

根性 *Konjou,* Willpower

Japanese people often use the word 根性 (*konjou*, will) along with がんばる (*ganbaru*, to give it one's all) [see Chapter 6-1] and 努力 (*doryoku*, efforts). *Konjou* is the will to stick with a task to the end, despite hardships or struggle.

Example 1

あの子はちょっと苦しいとすぐに練習をやめる。まったく根性がない。

*Ano ko wa chotto kurushii to sugu ni renshuu o yameru. Mattaku **konjou** ga nai.*
That kid bails on practicing for any lame excuse. He's got no guts.

Example 2

売り上げ目標を達成できないのは、根性が足りないからだ！

*Uriage mokuhyou o tassei dekinai no wa, **konjou ga tarinai** kara da!*
You can't reach the sales target because you lack the drive!

Konjou is commonly used in the world of sports. A player who sticks to a tough practice regimen is 根性がある人 (*konjou ga aru hito*, a person with guts), whereas a player who bails easily on the program is 根性がない人 (*konjou ga nai hito*, a wimp). During the training session, the sports director or a coach might say もっと根性を見せろ (*motto konjou o misero*, show me some heart), instead of がんばれ (*ganbare*, do your best).

Outside the world of sports, superiors used to blame subordinates, as shown in Example 2. If they failed to meet the goal, they were blamed for their lack of *konjou*. We believed we could accomplish anything through willpower alone, and this approach is called 根性論 (*konjouron*, the principle of never giving up).

Now, we place greater importance on practicality and efficiency, rather than laying success on individual efforts alone, so this approach is dying out. Still, the value of a person's determination remains deep within the Japanese psyche.

Example 3

勉強もしないでいい成績をとろうなんて、**根性の曲がった**考え方だ。

Benkyou mo shinaide ii seiseki o torou nante, **konjou no magatta** *kangaekata da.*

You have a twisted mind, if you think you can get good grades without studying.

Example 4

お前みたいな人間に教えてやることは何もない。**根性を入れ替えて**出直してこい！

Omae mitai na ningen ni oshiete yaru koto wa nani mo nai. **Konjou o irekaete** *denaoshite koi.*

I have nothing to teach people like you. Come back with a better attitude (swap out your crooked mentality).

Konjou was originally a Buddhist term, which indicated the nature of a person from birth. Even now, we refer to a person with bad personality as 根性が悪い (*konjou ga warui*, heart is bad, ill-natured) or 根性が曲がっている (*konjou ga magatte iru*, character is twisted). To correct someone's bad character at the root, we have expressions such as 根性をたたき直す (*konjou o tataki naosu*, to beat and fix one's bad nature, to reform one's character at boot camp) or 根性を入れ替える (*konjou o irekaeru*, to exchange one's character, to replace a bad nature with a good one). As you see, *konjou* represents a deeper element of human nature than the visible personality.

意地 (*iji*, will) is similar to *konjou*, but carries the image of obstinance or stubbornness. When a person clings to his opinions or attitude to the end, we say 男の意地を通す (*otoko no **iji o toosu***, a man who sticks to his guns) or 意地を張る (***iji o haru***, to never give in). Although both *konjou* and *iji* indicate the nature of a person who does not surrender amid adversity, *konjou* holds the more positive image of willpower stemming from a deep spirit.

A deeper look

スポ根 (*supokon*, sports and grit) is a genre of anime and TV drama in Japan. It is an abbreviation of スポーツ根性もの (*supootsu konjou mono*, the genre of sports and personal fortitude). We use the term in スポ根アニメ (*supokon anime*, sports-*konjou* anime) and スポ根ドラマ (*supokon dorama*, sports-*konjou* dramas). In most stories, the main character is an athlete with guts, who perseveres through strenuous training and countless hardships, ultimately to win in the endgame. We sometimes emphasize this word more and say ど根性 (*do konjou*, super guts).

At one point an ongoing study, 根性 (*konjou*), 努力 (*doryoku*, efforts) and 忍耐 (*nintai*, endurance) were ranked the top three on a list of favorite terms of Japanese people. Later, these kinds of words fell in rank, and softer terms, such as ありがとう (*arigatou*, thank you) and 思いやり (*omoiyari*, thoughtfulness, compassion) became more popular.

Likewise, the strict concept of *konjou-ron* has softened over the years. Nonetheless, in educating children at home and school, we still hold onto the importance of process over the results and of efforts over winning.

無理 *Muri*, Unreasonable

無理 (*muri*, impossible) is a combination of 無 (*mu*, not existent) and 理 (*ri*, reason), and means 道理が無い (*douri ga nai*, there is no reason). It refers to something that is unreasonable or illogical. 無理が通れば、道理がひっこむ (*muri ga tooreba, douri ga hikkomu*, where injustice passes, reason withdraws; where might is master, justice is servant) is a proverb in Japan. It means that if society accepts the unreasonable, people will stop doing the right thing.

Example 1

こんな成績では、親が心配するのも**無理**はない。

*Konna seiseki de wa, oya ga shinpai suru no mo **muri wa nai**.*

With such bad grades, no wonder the parents are worried.

Example 2

それは**無理**な相談だ。

*Sore wa **muri na** soudan da.*

That is a no-go. (The negotiation or proposal will never fly.)

Example 3

お忙しいのに**無理**を言ってすみません。

*Oisogashii noni **muri o itte** sumimasen.*

I'm sorry to ask so much at a busy time.

無理はない (*muri wa nai*, nothing unreasonable here) in Example 1 means 道理に合わないことではない (*douri ni awanai koto de wa nai*, it is not against reason, it is reasonable/understandable). Hence, the meanings are 当然だ (*touzen da*, it is natural) or もっともだ (*mottomo da*, it is quite right, no wonder). In Example 2, 無理 (*muri*) refers to something unreasonable, so he means that it is impossible to do.

As in Example 3, we use 無理を言う (*muri o iu*, request an unreasonable thing) when we require or ask someone to do the impossible. In most cases, we say 無理を言ってすみません (*muri o itte sumi masen*, sorry to ask the impossible) when we ask a favor.

Example 4

体の調子がよくないときは、あまり**無理**しないでください。

*Karada no choushi ga yokunai toki wa, amari **muri shinaide** kudasai.*

When you're in rough shape, please try not to do too much.

Example 5

少しぐらい**無理**してでも、絶対にこの仕事は最後までやり遂げたい。

*Sukoshi gurai **muri shite demo**, zettai ni kono shigoto wa saigo made yaritoge tai.*

I may be overdoing it, but I definitely want to finish this work.

Example 6

ちょっと**無理**し過ぎなんじゃない？　たまには休んだら？

*Chotto **muri shisugi** nan ja nai? Tamani wa yasundara?*

Aren't you overdoing it? Why not take an occasional break?

When we make excessive efforts to achieve something challenging, we call it 無理する (*muri suru*, to do the undoable).

We say 無理しないでください (*muri shinaide kudasai*, please don't overdo it) to encourage or comfort someone, instead of がんばってください (*ganbatte kudasai*, please do your best). It is a gentler way to talk to someone in a place of hardship or a difficult situation. That person could reply with 少しぐらい無理してでもがんばります (*sukoshi gurai muri shite demo ganbari masu*, even though I may overdo it a little, I'll try my best). Japanese people favor this kind of response because we value *doryoku* (efforts) and *konjou* (guts) [see Chapter 6-2].

Refer to "A deeper look" in Chapter 6-1 to see how Japanese companies struggle to balance overwork with the private life for employees.

修行 *Shugyou*, Training, Ascetic Practices

修行 (*shugyou*, training) was originally a Buddhist term. It refers to the rigorous training practiced by monks seeking enlightenment. For example, they may take extended treks to deep mountains or meditate for hours sitting under a waterfall.

It is also used to describe the intensive training involved in mastering arts, technical skills, and academic disciplines.

Example 1

一人前の寿司職人になるためには、少なくとも十年間は**修行**が必要だ。

*Ichininmae no sushi shokunin ni naru tame ni wa, sukunakutomo juunenkan wa **shugyou** ga hitsuyou da.*

To become a full-fledged sushi chef, you must train at least ten years.

The word 修行 (*shugyou*, training) has a stricter image than 練習 (*renshuu*, practice) and トレーニング (*toreeningu*, training). When we hear 料理の練習 (*ryouri no renshuu*, cooking practice) and 料理の修行 (*ryouri no shugyou*, cooking training), we imagine different practice environments. *Shugyou* is much harder and intense than *renshuu*, and it carries the element of spiritual training.

Artisans learn not only technique from their masters, but also the spiritual mindset. Training encompasses many long years before they become independent, and disciples may even live with their masters to emerge themselves in the study. Hence, the term *shugyou* is appropriate to describe this kind of training.

Example 2

その音楽家は、ヨーロッパで二年間の**武者修行**をし、音楽家としての腕をさらに磨いた。

*Sono ongakuka wa, yooroppa de ninenkan no **musha shugyou** o shi, ongakuka to shite no ude o sarani migaita.*

That musician underwent strict training in Europe for two years and significantly polished his technique.

武者 (*musha*) is a warrior. In Example 2, the speaker used 武者修行 (***musha shugyou***, warrior/arduous training) instead of 勉強 (*benkyou*, study) to underscore the effort and hardships endured in Europe. We can also assume that the musician grew spiritually from the experience.

Some young people choose to forgo a comfortable life in Japan and experience the challenging environment of an unfamiliar language and culture. They say 海外に武者修行に行く (*kaigai ni musha shugyou ni iku*, I'm going abroad as a training [to open my mind and toughen up]). Unfortunately, some end up finding an easier life there, abandoning the primary purpose of *shugyou*.

Since proper training is considered requisite to success, we can even mock a person for any mistake, by saying 修行が足りない (***shugyou ga tarinai***, training is insufficient).

Example 3

そんな簡単なこともわからないなんて、まだまだ**修行が足りない**ね。

*Sonna kantan na koto mo wakaranai nante, madamada **shugyou ga tarinai** ne.*

If you don't get this easy thing, you've got a long way to go (in your training).

In Example 3, the statement does not mean that the person literally needs to go off and redo training. It is used as a light joke, expressing that the person needs to study or practice more.

精進 (*shoujin*, devotion to one's research) is similar to ***shugyou*** and it also comes from a Buddhist term.

In Buddhism, it is forbidden to kill animals. Therefore, Buddhist practitioners eschew meat of any kind. They eat only vegetables to keep their body and mind pure and focus on their training. We called this action 精進 (*shoujin*).

Even now, when we hold Buddhist funerals in Japan, we eat meatless dishes made with vegetables and tofu. This cuisine is called 精進料理 (*shoujin ryouri*, the cuisine of Buddhist training). Then, when the period of 精進 (*shoujin*) is over, we can return to a life of meat and *sake*. We call this shift, 精進落とし (*shoujin otoshi*, dropping the Buddhist diet, a return to meat or alcohol after a period of self-denial).

精進する (*shoujin suru*, to stay pure and focus on training) was first meant to indicate the efforts to seek Buddhist enlightenment, following strict rules of abstention. Over time, we came to use the term to indicate the pains we take to achieve any large goal.

A master might say to his apprentice, だいぶ腕を上げてきたが、一人前の職人になるためには、もう少し精進しないといけないな (*daibu ude o agete kita ga, ichininmae no shokunin ni naru tame ni wa, mou sukoshi shoujin shinai to ikenai na*, You have improved, but to become a full-fledged artisan, you need to train harder). 精進 (*shoujin*) holds the image of serious dedication to a task, and working without any distraction.

To sum up, the long period of apprenticeship to become an artisan or to master a discipline is 修行 (*shugyou*). Following a strict, self-imposed regimen to achieve any large goal is 精進 (*shoujin*).

武士道 *Bushidou*, The Way of the Warrior

In 1603, Ieyasu Tokugawa unified Japan, and the Edo period (1603–1868) began. During this long era, there were no significant wars, so samurai warriors no longer had to be ready to fight to the death. Essentially, their purpose was to do battle with enemies of their master, so they were not prepared to live in a peaceful world. Since they wished to retain their status in society and maintain honor as before, they developed an ideal image of the warrior, which became a spiritual path. We call that 武士道 (*bushidou*, the way of the warrior).

Example 1

現代の日本人は、武士道の精神を失ったと言われている。

*Gendai no nihonjin wa, **bushidou no seishin** o ushinatta to iwarete iru.*

It is said that modern Japanese people have lost their warrior spirit.

Example 2

死を恐れないのが武士道だと言われてきた。

*Shi o osorenai no ga **bushidou** da to iwarete kita.*

We used to say that to be unafraid of death was the way of the warrior.

武士道 (*bushidou*) is the righteous way to live as a warrior. For instance, *bushi* (warriors) must be ready to stand up against anything without fearing death, and must never do shameful things to keep their honorable status in society. Lying, deceiving someone, and committing cowardly acts for their own benefit are considered violations of *bushidou*.

Example 3

A この補償金(ほしょうきん)は会社(かいしゃ)が払(はら)うようにするから、君(きみ)は払(はら)わなくていいよ。

Kono hoshoukin wa kaisha ga harau you ni suru kara, kimi wa harawanakute ii yo.

I'll have the company handle the compensation (for your mistake), so you don't have to pay it.

B 本当(ほんとう)にいいんですか？

Hontou ni iin desu ka?

Is that all right?

A 大丈夫(だいじょうぶ)。**武士(ぶし)に二言(にごん)はない**よ。

*Daijoubu. **Bushi ni nigon wa nai** yo.*

No problem. I have spoken (a promise is a promise).

武士(ぶし)に二言(にごん)はない (*bushi ni nigon wa nai*, a warrior does not speak twice, a warrior keeps his word once spoken and never makes an excuse). 武士(ぶし)は食(く)わねど、高楊枝(たかようじ) (*bushi wa kuwane do, takayouji*, a warrior uses a toothpick even if he did not eat; a true warrior will not display hunger, instead, pretending he just ate by brandishing a toothpick). These are expressions we still use today.

Samurai during the Edo period served as officials of the main or regional governments. They were not wealthy, because they received only ungenerous amounts of rice as salary. However, they were raised to uphold an honorable life, which would be respected by the lower rank of farmers and merchants. So, according to *bushidou*, it was considered shameful if they talked about money or complained about their poverty.

Even though the warrior class was outlawed in the Meiji period (1868–1912), the philosophy of *bushidou* remained in the public mind. The concept was widely popularized when educator, philosopher, and politician Inazo Nitobe (1862–1933) wrote *Bushido: The Soul of Japan* (1899) in the English language. The book was highly appraised abroad, causing Japanese people to reassess the value of *bushidou*.

The word *bushi* came from the mid-Heian period (794–1185) to define the warriors in feudal Japan. Groups of farmers and landowners began to practice their sword skills to protect their own or their master's property from invaders. In 1185, 源氏 (*Genji*, the Minamoto clan) won over 平家 (*Heike*, the Taira clan). The Minamoto clan was a group of warriors from east, and the Taira were attached to the emperor and royal families in the west. Having superior military strength, the Minamoto clan fought and won over the Taira clan, and ruled the entirety of Japan, with the 将軍 (*shougun*, military leader) at the top. With the establishment of the hereditary dictatorship of 鎌倉幕府 (*Kamakura bakufu*, the Kamakura shogunate, 1185–1333) by the Minamoto clan, political power shifted from the emperor and his nobles to the *samurai* class. *Samurai* were *bushi* warriors that held high social status and sworn allegiance to a lord. That structure, ruled by **bushi**, continued for 700 years, until the end of the Edo period (mid-19th century).

The core purpose of *bushi* was to fight to the death for their master, who bestowed their property. It was a relationship of give and take. 一所懸命 (*issho kenmei*, risking life to protect territory) came from that duty. Now, that concept is altered slightly to the commonly used expression 一生懸命 (*isshou kenmei*, risking life like there's no tomorrow, to try one's utmost).

In the Edo period, when *bushi* lost their identity as fighters, they took on the responsibility of governing. During that era, the precepts of 儒学 (*jugaku*, Confucianism from China) were greatly respected. From Confucianism, the concept of 忠 (*chuu*, loyalty to serve their master unconditionally) was promoted to maintain peace. This caused the *bushi* to question his warrior identity again. For them, it was an existential dilemma, so they focused on the moral codes of *bushidou*. Hence, throughout the Edo period, the honorable *bushi* continued to train in swordsmanship and archery, and declared their resolve to die for their masters, even when there was little to no threat of war.

❁ 武士道は死ぬことと見つけたり

Bushidou wa shinu koto to mitsuketari.

(The true meaning of) *bushidou* lies in dying.

This is a famous quote from 葉隠 *Hagakure* [Hidden by the Leaves], a collection of thoughts, sayings, and anecdotes that illustrate the values of *bushidou*, written in the mid-Edo period. The quote states that dying for one's master is the ultimate statement of *bushidou*.

In his book, *Bushido: The Soul of Japan*, Inazo Nitobe explained the status of *bushi* using the French term, "*noblesse oblige.*" He emphasized that *bushi*, as people of honor and noble rank, had a solemn responsibility and obligation to support society.

Chapter 7
日本人の価値観
Nihonjin no Kachikan
Japanese Values

品 *Hin*, Class

To assess the quality of things, we use adjectives such as 良い (*yoi*, good) and 悪い (*warui*, bad). Referring to the quality itself, we use the word 品 (*hin*, class). So, we would say 品がある (**hin ga aru**, to have class, to be classy) and 品がない (**hin ga nai**, to have no class).

Other words using *hin* include 上品 (*jouhin*, sophisticated), 下品 (*gehin*, vulgar), 品位 (*hin'i*, grace), 品格 (*hinkaku*, dignity) and 品性 (*hinsei*, character). They are used to evaluate people's attitudes, actions, or the appearance of things.

Example 1

あの女優は、話し方に品があって好感が持てる。

*Ano joyuu wa, hanashikata ni **hin ga atte** koukan ga moteru.*

That actress gives us good impression because of her refined manner of speaking.

Example 2

彼女はハンバーガーを食べるときでも上品に食べる。

*Kanojo wa hanbaagaa o taberu toki demo **jouhin** ni taberu.*

She is graceful, even when eating a hamburger.

Example 3

そんな下品なテレビ番組を見るんじゃありません！

*Sonna **gehin na** terebi bangumi o mirun ja ari masen!*

Don't watch such a crude TV program!

When we hear 彼女は品がある (*kanojo wa hin ga aru*, she has class), we can imagine different looks for her. However, 品 (***hin***) does not designate someone's superficial appearance. Rather, it refers to internal elegance, which could manifest through language, attitude, and actions.

On the other hand, we say 品がない (*hin ga nai,* having no class), 下品だ (*gehin da,* to be vulgar), 品位に欠ける (*hin'i ni kakeru,* to lack class), and 品格がない (*hinkaku ga nai*, lacking grace), to describe a person who speaks loudly or displays open emotion in public, brags about personal wealth, brings up obscene topics, or has any attitude that is repulsive.

Hin ga aru can also refer to objects. For instance, we use that to describe clothes, paintings, or cups to praise them.

Example 4

この着物は、ほかのと比べてデザインは地味だが、**品があって**美しい。

Kono kimono wa, hoka no to kurabete dezain wa jimi da ga, ***hin ga atte*** *utsukushii.*

The design of this *kimono* is simpler than the others, but it has a refined beauty.

Example 5

部屋に飾る絵は、派手なものよりも、**品があって**飽きないものがいい。

Heya ni kazaru e wa, hade na mono yori mo, ***hin ga atte*** *akinai mono ga ii.*

When selecting a painting for a room, in lieu of some gaudy thing, it should be something elegant that you will never tire of.

Japanese people normally prefer to be humble and restrained [see Chapter 5-1]. We suppress our emotions, avoid asserting our own opinions, and generally conduct ourselves with reservation [see Chapter 3-1]. In addition, we prefer the simple and plain over colorful and flashy things, like gold [see Chapter 7-3].

That sense of sublime value is expressed with the word 品 (*hin*). *Hin* engenders a gentle or pleasant feeling that is born naturally from the inner beauty, manifest in a person's attitude or gestures, or the quiet quality of a fine object. Japanese people would be delighted to be praised with *hin ga aru* and feel denigrated by the criticism of *hin ga nai* or *gehin da*.

The adjective おくゆかしい (***okuyukashii***, drawn to look deeper, restrained, refined) is similar to 品がある (*hin ga aru*). Japanese people think it vulgar to expose emotions and desires without restraint. おくゆかしい (*okuyukashii*) is used to describe a person who can control his emotions and is considerate of the feelings of others around him. The person has a quiet and sublime center, which draws people in.

In contrast, when we criticize a vulgar attitude, we use the adjective はしたない (***hashitanai***, lowly, ill-mannered). For example, it would apply to an adult crying loudly in public or hogging the expensive foods at the buffet. Japanese people disdain exposing emotions that should be controlled and indulging desires that should remain hidden.

やまとなでしこ
Yamato Nadeshiko, The Japanese Ideal Woman

The Japan National Women's Football Team achieved world fame when they won the FIFA Women's World Cup Final in 2011. The team is known by its nickname なでしこジャパン (*Nadeshiko Japan*), and the Japan Women's Soccer League is called also なでしこリーグ (*Nadeshiko Riigu*, the *Nadeshiko* League). *Nadeshiko* is borrowed from the term, やまとなでしこ (*yamato nadeshiko*, ancient Japan's fringed pink flower), which is used to symbolize an idealized image of a Japanese woman.

やまと (大和) (*yamato*) is a term for ancient Japan. We now use the name to indicate something that has existed since then. For instance, 大和言葉 (*yamato kotoba*, *yamato* words) refers to Old Japanese, and 大和魂 (*yamato damashii*, the *yamato* spirit) indicates the Japanese people's essential morality and spirit.

やまとなでしこ (*yamato nadeshiko*) is originally a wildflower, and we also call it, simply なでしこ (*nadeshiko*). In early summer, it produces small and delicate flowers with a light pink color. Japanese people apply the image of this pure and gentle flower to the image of the ideal young woman, and began to use it as a synonym.

Example 1

彼女こそ、まさに**やまとなでしこ**、すばらしい人だ。

*Kanojo koso, masani **yamato nadeshiko**, subarashii hito da.*
She is truly a *yamato nadeshiko*, an exquisite person.

One trait of the Japanese ideal woman is しとやかさ (*shitoyakasa*, gracefulness). しとやか (***shitoyaka***) indicates a woman, whose language, attitudes and character are calm, and who has a humble and graceful presence. In the past, しとやかさ (*shitoyakasa*) was listed as a requirement for an ideal future wife.

Example 2

結婚するなら、**しとやか**で家庭的な女性がいいです。

*Kekkon suru nara, **shitoyaka** de katei teki na josei ga ii desu.*
If I were to get married, I would prefer a graceful and home-oriented woman.

In the past, foreign men considered the pure, graceful Japanese woman to be the perfect wife. Now, women's social advancement has progressed, and the social evaluation of women has diversified. Hence, the criteria of the Japanese ideal women as しとやか (*shitoyaka*) does not necessarily stand.

Nevertheless, *yamato nadeshiko* persists as the image of the Japanese ideal woman, who displays the feminine virtues of old Japan.

派手・地味 *Hade and Jimi*, Flashy and Plain

7-3

We call clear, bright colors, such as red, yellow, and blue, 派手な色 (*hade na iro*, vibrant colors). When clothes are colorful or have eye-catching designs, we call them 派手な服 (*hade na fuku*, flashy clothes). Hence, 派手 (***hade***) characterizes something that grabs people's attention, and we use the term to describe people's appearance, attitude, or actions.

Example 1

彼はいつも派手なことばかりするので、上司はいつもひやひやしている。

*Kare wa itsumo **hade na** koto bakari suru node, joushi wa itsumo hiyahiya shite iru.*

He always makes a spectacle of himself, and it always gives his boss the cold sweats.

Example 2

芸能人は生活が派手だと思われているが、みながそうとは限らない。

*Geinoujin wa seikatsu ga **hade da** to omowarete iru ga, mina ga sou to wa kagiranai.*

We assume people in the entertainment world have a lavish lifestyle, but not everyone does.

Below are some expressions using *hade*.

❀ 派手なこと (*hade na koto*, a spectacle, an incident that catches people's attention)

❀ 派手な生活 (*hade na seikatsu*, an extravagant life, a lavish or ostentatious lifestyle)

❀ 派手な性格 (*hade na seikaku*, a flamboyant, theatrical personality)

Hade usually carries a negative image when describing a person. It implies that he does not hide his emotions and always blurts out his opinions. Japanese people feel a person like this should be *hikaeme* (restrained) [see Chapter 5-1].

The antonym of 派手 (***hade***) is 地味 (***jimi***, plain). It indicates something that is subdued or restrained in appearance.

In books on business etiquette, we can get advice, such as 会社では派手なお化粧は避けましょう (*kaisha de wa hade na okeshou wa sake mashou*, avoid too much make-up at work) or スーツは地味な色のものを選びましょう (*suutsu wa jimi na iro no mono o erabi mashou*, select plain colored suits). In some cases, we may intentionally choose something eye-catching to make a strong impression, but, in the Japanese business world, we prefer a plain and inconspicuous outfit.

In Japan, we tend to favor *jimi* (the subdued) over *hade* (the swanky). Still, in cases where we wish to demonstrate positive aggressiveness or make a fashion statement, we would need to make a splash. If someone says あの人って地味だよね (*ano hito tte **jimi da yone***, he just fades into the background), or if someone tells us その洋服ちょっと地味じゃない？ (*sono youfuku chotto **jimi ja nai?***, That outfit is a bit too plain), we know that *jimi* can reflect disapproval of the person or his clothes, based on the context.

渋い (***shibui***, astringent) is similar to 地味 (***jimi***). Its first meaning refers to the bitterness of green tea or an unripe persimmon. However, when we use it to describe things or people, it implies that they have an elegant value, veiled, tranquil, and with depth. For instance, we use it as 渋い色 (*shibui iro*, a subtle color), 渋いファッション (*shibui fasshon*, chic fashion), 渋い男性 (*shibui dansei*, a suave gentleman), and 渋い生き方 (*shibui ikikata*, a chic lifestyle).

Example 3

若いのにバッハが好きだなんて、なかなか渋いね。
Wakai noni Bahha ga suki da nante, nakanaka **shibui** *ne.*
At your age, an appreciation of Bach is pretty cool.

In Example 3, the youngster is praised for having sophisticated taste (*shibui*), when people of that age usually like loud pop music (*hade*).

Since Japanese people value simple, unadorned things, we have descriptive words to praise people and things. We use 素朴 (*soboku*, simple), 飾り気がない (*kazarike ga nai*, unadorned, plain), 品がいい (*hin ga ii*, classy), and 上品 (*jouhin*, high class) [see Chapter 7-1].

In the world of Japanese traditional culture, including Japanese-style painting and tea ceremony, modesty and simplicity receive higher esteem than something garish and glittery. When introducing Japanese culture to foreign visitors, we might take them to traditional sites, such as tea houses, stone gardens, or old and quiet temples. The aesthetic value they provide is called わび・さび (***wabi-sabi***, a taste for simplicity, tranquility, and subdued refinement).

Wabi and *sabi* are often put together as a set phrase, but their meanings differ slightly. わび (***wabi***) in modern language is seen in the adjective わびしい (*wabishii*, dismayed, desolate, forlorn, inconsolable). It used to hold the negative image of poor, shabby, and something lacking. Later, as expressed in the worlds of 茶道 (*sadou*, tea ceremony) and 俳句 (*haiku*, a Japanese poetry genre in syllables of five-seven-five), a new aesthetic value emerged that prized the beauty of simplicity and grace over the ostentatious and gaudy. Consequently, we began to value *wabi*.

Similarly, さび (***sabi***) in modern language is related to 寂しい (*sabishii*, lonely) and 寂れる (*sabireru*, to be deserted). It presents an image of a desolate place, stillness, and loneliness. Nevertheless, people found the true beauty and humanity in a secluded life and in old or withered things. We called that *sabi*.

Japanese people see the value of *wabi* (the incomplete) and *sabi* (the impermanent). We treasure old, simple, quiet, and natural things and discovering their true beauty. *Wabi* and *sabi* are key concepts that speak to the aesthetic values of Japan.

A deeper look

Buddhist monk and renowned essayist, Kenko Yoshida, wrote 徒然草 *Tsurezuregusa* [Essays in Idleness] in the late Kamakura period. In this book, we find the following sentence.

花はさかりに、月はくまなきをのみ見るものかは

Hana wa sakari ni, tsuki wa kumanaki o nomi miru mono ka wa

Why should we appreciate only the cherry blossom at full bloom and the moon at its fullest?

From ancient times, Japanese people have found beauty in things that are imperfect and transitory.

Likewise, we can praise an older gentleman as いぶし銀のような味がある (*ibushi gin no you na aji ga aru*, charming as matte silver). ***Ibushi gin*** ("oxidized" silver) is silver treated with a sulfur compound to remove the shine. So here, the man looks ordinary at first sight but reveals hidden qualities and charm. This kind of compliment reveals the Japanese preference for people or things that look *jimi* (plain) over those that look *hade* (shiny).

茶の湯 (*cha no yu*, tea gathering) was introduced from the Song dynasty of China (960–1279). Originally, it simply meant to invite people to your home and serve tea. In Japan, the practice developed, becoming deeply connected with the simplicity of Zen philosophy and the spirit of *bushi*, searching for the perfect path between life and death. Thus, it was elevated to the art of 茶道 (*sadou*, the way of tea, tea ceremony) and embodied the aesthetics of *wabi-sabi*.

Daisetsu Suzuki (1870–1966), a scholar of Zen philosophy, introduced the Zen culture of Japan to the world. In his work, *Zen Buddhism and Its Influence on Japanese Culture*, he defines *wabi-sabi* as an aesthetic appreciation of poverty.

We say 清貧に甘んずる (***seihin ni amanzuru***, to be content with poverty). It suggests that leading a pure and proper life in poverty is preferable to an extravagant life absorbed in moneymaking. This illustrates our respect for the ethic of *wabi-sabi*.

恩・義理 *On and Giri,* Debt of Gratitude and Sense of Obligation

Japanese people typically carry an acute awareness of obligation. We constantly assess the degrees of indebtedness, weighing favors we did for certain people against those they did for us. Even weeks after the fact, we feel compelled to express gratitude for the kindness done for us. Foreigners might be surprised to see the extent to which we hold onto our past debts of gratitude. Nevertheless, we try never to forget someone who did a favor for us. That is called 恩 (*on*, debt of gratitude).

Dependent on the degree of debt to a person, we would need to give back お返し (*okaeshi*, a return gift or gesture). We could send a present or help the person when in a time of trouble. We call that 恩返し (*on gaeshi*, repayment for kindness). If we fail to demonstrate our gratitude properly, we will be harshly criticized as 恩知らず (*on shirazu*, ungrateful).

Example 1

早く自立して、今まで育ててくれた両親に恩返しがしたい。

*Hayaku jiritsu shite, ima made sodatete kureta ryoushin ni **on gaeshi** ga shi tai.*

I hope to become independent as soon as possible and give back to the parents who raised me.

Example 2

お世話になった人を裏切るなんて、なんて恩知らずなやつだ。

*Osewa ni natta hito o uragiru nante, nante **on shirazu** na yatsu da.*

To betray the very person who took care of him—what an ungrateful bastard!

We believe we need to repay any significant act of kindness. The feeling of moral debt is called 義理 (**giri**, obligation). We say 義理がある (*giri ga aru*, to have obligation to someone) or 恩義がある (*ongi ga aru*, to be deeply indebted to someone).

Example 3

あの人には**義理がある**ので、頼みを断れない。

*Ano hito ni wa **giri ga aru** node, tanomi o kotowarenai.*

I owe him a debt of gratitude, so I cannot refuse his request.

義理 (*giri*) originally referred to the righteous beliefs in respecting the rules of society. When we use the word in daily life, the belief is applied to the maintenance of relationships.

Example 4

後輩の吉田君はとても**義理堅**くて、旅行に行くと必ずおみやげを買ってきてくれる。

*Kouhai no Yoshida-kun wa totemo **giri gatakute**, ryokou ni iku to kanarazu omiyage o katte kite kureru.*

Mr. Yoshida, a junior in the office, has a strong sense of duty and always brings me a travel gift.

In Example 4, Mr. Yoshida is praised as 義理堅い (*giri gatai*, giri is solid, having a strong sense of obligation). On the other hand, if we failed to repay the kindness of someone, we would be judged to be 礼儀を知らない (*reigi o shiranai*, not knowing manners, uncouth) [see Chapter 4-3]. In Japanese society, one's awareness of obligation can be critical.

Example 5

忙しさのあまり、お世話になった人にずっと連絡ができずに義理を欠いている。

*Isogashisa no amari, osewa ni natta hito ni zutto renraku ga dekizu ni **giri o kaite iru**.*

Due to a demanding schedule, I have fallen out of touch with a person who has taken great care of me. I am remiss in my obligations.

Failing to fulfill a promise or neglecting a primary relationship is called 義理を欠く (***giri o kaku***, to lack *giri*, to be derelict in obligation to someone). Japanese people place great importance on wedding ceremonies and funerals. We must carefully follow the requisite rules and habits for these occasions and never fail to carry out our obligations to others. For example, if someone who had taken care of us passed away, we must, by all means, attend the funeral and offer an envelope of money. Also, it is important to send a gift as soon as we hear that a valued person, or close relative of that person, is getting married or having a baby.

Japanese weddings are notorious for the expensive ご祝儀 (*goshuugi*, gift money) required. *Goshuugi* is set in large, fixed amounts, depending on various factors. In our late twenties or early thirties, a lot of our friends get married, so we have to attend multiple weddings. Consequently, we can become ご祝儀貧乏 (*goshuugi binbou*, poor due to wedding gift money). However, even if we are financially tight, we must not refuse the wedding invitation, unless there is a serious emergency.

A deeper look

In Japan, on Valentine's Day (February 14), it is customary for a woman to give chocolates to her special man (whereas, men usually do the gift-giving in Western countries). On that day, women also give chocolates to their male friends, family members, or superiors at their workplace. That chocolate is called 義理チョコ (***giri choko***, obligation chocolate). It does not mean they like these men romantically, but it is a social obligation that women do.

The word 義理 (***giri***) carries the nuance of requisite duty or something that we do because we feel obligated. It does not necessarily come from true gratitude.

There is an expression 義理と人情の板挟み (***giri to ninjou no itabasami***, crushed between duty and sentiment). For example, if someone caught a thief and then discovered it was his son, he naturally would not want to see his loved one become a criminal by turning him in. However, if he let his son go, that would go against his duty to society. So, he would feel torn, choosing between the love for his son and the obligations of society.

In Japanese traditional theater genres, such as *kabuki*, we have countless stories based on the theme of *giri* and *ninjou* (compassion). That reflects how *giri* can come into conflict with *ninjou* in our daily lives.

いさぎよい *Isagiyoi*, Gallant, Sportsmanlike

7-5

On Japanese television, we are used to seeing a company president bowing deeply and apologizing publicly for any exposed scandal perpetrated by his company. We likely would not see this scene often in other countries. There, they might think it better not to apologize, because it could place their company at a legal disadvantage, or they might explain the circumstances first and apologize later.

In Japan, if there is any culpability at all, we believe that it is always better to admit responsibility and to apologize sincerely without excuse or explanation. We call this attitude いさぎよい (*isagiyoi*, gallant). Contrarily, if one gives detailed excuses and does not apologize for the wrongdoing, we would call that attitude いさぎよくない (*isagiyokunai*, in bad form, unsportsmanlike). That kind of behavior would be unforgivable, and would only serve to further anger the harmed parties.

Example 1

その会社の社長は、自社に責任があることを**いさぎよく**認めて、謝罪した。

*Sono kaisha no shachou wa, jisha ni sekinin ga aru koto o **isagiyoku** mitomete, shazai shita.*

The president of that company gracefully admitted their responsibility and rendered an official apology.

Example 2

試合に負けて言い訳をするなんて、**いさぎよくない**。

Shiai ni makete iiwake o suru nante, ***isagiyokunai****.*
It is bad form to make excuses when we lose a game.

Some years ago, there was an elevator accident in Tokyo, and a high school student lost his life. The elevator maker was a foreign company, and the president was not Japanese. His response was to speak to the Japanese media, where he explained the cause of the accident in detail before issuing a formal apology more than a week later. From the Japanese perspective, his explanation only was heard as a feeble justification, and he was gravely condemned.

いさぎよさ (*isagiyosa*, resolute composure, manliness) was thought to be extremely valuable during the *bushi* (warrior) era [see Chapter 6-5].

The duty of warriors was to fight for their master, and if they lost, the only honorable consequence was to die. According to *bushidou* (the warrior's code), fleeing or asking mercy from an enemy were deemed extremely dishonorable.

The most extreme example of *isagiyosa* was the notorious practice of 切腹 (*seppuku*, suicide by slicing open his abdomen). A warrior who made an egregious error or did not fulfill his responsibility should commit *seppuku* without reluctance. That would be the only way to keep his honor.

To most Japanese people, 桜の花 (*sakura no hana*, cherry blossoms) comes to mind as an image of a valiant act. Cherry blossoms perish as soon as they reach full bloom. Compared to other flowers that bloom for some time, we consider cherry blossoms to be gallant, because the petals let go and fly away without hesitation after revealing their full colors. It is one reason Japanese people appreciate cherry blossoms and revel in the yearly cherry blossom festivals.

In Japan, even for minor infractions, citizens will call for politicians to resign immediately. We believe that they should not make excuses or stick to their political positions. They must resign righteously, which is seen as けじめ (*kejime*, a clean break from the past) [see Chapter 1-4].

A deeper look

We can say that いさぎよさ (*isagiyosa*, resolute composure, manliness) was the most important principle in the moral codes of Japanese warriors.

The duty of the warrior was to fight, and the best image of the warrior was to fight without fear of death. Therefore, if one is unlucky enough to lose after valiant efforts to win, he should choose an honorable death rather than fleeing or pleading for his life. We praised this brave quality as *isagiyoi*.

In *The Chrysanthemum and the Sword*, American anthropologist Ruth Benedict (1887–1948) explained the Japanese no-surrender policy in the chapter, "The Japanese in the War." She noted that Japanese people deemed it cowardly that the American forces installed safety devices in bomber planes during World War II. She pointed out that, for the Japanese, the ultimate honor was to die for their country.

もったいない *Mottainai,* Wasteful

When throwing away a carton of milk that went bad after drinking only a small portion, we regret wasting the milk by not finishing it in time. When discarding a shirt because of a small stain, we regret losing a good piece of clothing by not being more careful.

That feeling of regret for waste in Japanese is もったいない（*mottainai,* wasteful）.

Example 1

このパソコン、まだ動くのに処分するなんて、もったいない。

Kono pasokon, mada ugoku noni shobun suru nante, ***mottainai***.

This personal computer is still running. It's a shame to scrap something that still works.

Example 2

こんなに涼しいのにクーラーをつけるなんてもったいない。

Konnani suzushii noni kuuraa o tsukeru nante ***mottainai***.

When it's this cool outside, it's a waste to turn on the A/C.

Example 3

試験の前なので、おしゃべりする時間ももったいないと思う。

Shiken no mae na node, oshaberi suru jikan mo ***mottainai*** *to omou.*

With the exam looming, it's stupid to fritter away time gabbing with friends.

We say もったいない (*mottainai*, wasteful) when we feel regret wasting food we could still eat or losing practical things we could still use. We warn ourselves not to squander equipment in Example 1, electricity in Example 2, and study time in Example 3.

In older times, we were warned not to waste money and to value all things. For example, in an ordinary family, we used to adopt the clothes that our older siblings wore. We called that お下がり (*osagari*, hand-me-downs). It comes from the ethic that we must make full use of things. Back then, our parents told us not to waste even a grain of rice. Farmers broke their backs cultivating rice, so we were taught to honor their hard work by eating every morsel in our bowl.

Mottainai is also used when referring to the qualities of people.

Example 4

彼は優秀な社員なのに、コピーの仕事しかさせないなんて、実にもったいない。

Kare wa yuushuu na shain na noni, kopii no shigoto shika sasenai nante, jitsuni mottainai.

He's an excellent employee. What a waste to give him only copy work.

In Example 4, they lament that his capabilities are underutilized in the company.

As you see, *mottainai* is used as a warning or criticism when wasting a thing or a person. However, *mottainai* has a different function in the following examples.

Example 5

あの奥(おく)さんは、彼(かれ)にはもったいないようなすばらしい人(ひと)だ。

*Ano okusan wa, kare ni wa **motttainai** you na subarashii hito da.*
His wife is a wonderful person. She's way too good for him.

Example 6

こんな高価(こうか)なお品(しな)をいただいて、私(わたし)にはもったいない。

*Konna kouka na oshina o itadaite, watashi ni wa **mottainai**.*
This is such a luxurious gift. I don't deserve it.

In Example 5, it appears that he is badmouthing the man by comparing him to his wonderful wife, and it can hold that meaning. However, the speaker is actually focused on praising the qualities of his wife.

Example 6 is a common expression that we use to express gratitude for a present. We compare our humble status with the extravagance of the gift, and state that the quality of such a present is bound to be wasted on us. It certainly is an unusual way to express appreciation for a gift.

A deeper look

In Japan, the population is large, and the landmass is small. Since we have limited natural resources and space for agriculture, it became necessary to treasure all things in daily life. As a result, we disdain wasting things and not making proper use of our resources. This is the background from which *mottainai* was born.

Historically, we did not have a wide tradition of eating meat other than fish, so the Japanese diet was not rich, because Buddhism taught us that 殺(せっ)

生 (*sesshou*, killing animals, especially four-legged animals) is a sin. From the frugal management of scarcity, Japanese utilized the resources they had at hand to get complex nutrients from sources other cultures might not consider, such as seaweed, root vegetables, and wild greens. Ironically, from a place of scarcity, the Japanese traditional diet came to be considered one of the healthiest in the world.

Furthermore, the principles of frugality and treasuring what we have align with the moral codes of *bushi* (warriors), who accepted their meager lives without complaint [see Chapter 6-5]. The philosophy of 清貧 (*seihin*, honorable poverty) in *wabi-sabi* (aesthetic value in simplicity) is also closely tied to the Japanese appreciation of treasuring what we have and not wasting it [see Chapter 7-3] .

This Japanese word *mottainai* is usually translated as "wasteful" in English. However, the Japanese term has a different nuance. As Assistant Minister in the Ministry for Environment and Natural Resources for Kenya, Nobel peace prize laureate Wangarī Maathai (1940 – 2011) was struck by the term, *mottainai*, when she visited Japan in 2005. She found that the term encapsulated in one word the three principles of waste-reduction: "Reduce, Reuse, and Recycle," or "the 3Rs." She then became a passionate activist of waste reduction, and advocated the 3Rs to the world using *mottainai* as a slogan. Following that, the Japanese 2005 Annual Report on the Environment advocated the spirit of *mottainai*. The report pointed out that *mottainai* not only holds the meaning of regret for lost resources, it also stresses that the principal value or role of resources is better utilized.

Nowadays, the word *mottainai* is frequently used in songs and books, and the concept has supported the global concerns of food loss. "MOTTAINAI" is now a meme that is spreading around the world.

Everyday Conversations 5: Apology First and Foremost

すみません (*sumi masen*, I'm sorry)

Discussion in the office:

課長： 鈴木君、ちょっと…
Kachou: Suzuki-kun, chotto...
Section Chief: Mr. Suzuki. May I speak with you a moment?

鈴木： はい、何でしょうか。
Suzuki: Hai, nan deshou ka.
Suzuki: Yes, what is it?

課長： この書類、君のハンコがないよ。
Kachou: Kono shorui, kimi no hanko ga nai yo.
Section chief: Look at this document. You did not stamp it with your seal.

鈴木： あ、失礼しました！
Suzuki: A, **shitsurei shi mashita**!
Suzuki: Oh, I do apologize.

課長： これじゃ、部長のところに持って行けないじゃないか。
Kachou: Kore ja, buchou no tokoro ni motte ikenai ja nai ka.
Section chief: I cannot bring it to the director like this.

鈴木： **すみません**、ちょっと急いでいたもので…
Suzuki: **Sumi masen**, chotto isoide ita mono de...
Suzuki: I'm so sorry; I was in a bit of a hurry...

課長：いつも言っているじゃないか、書類には必ずハンコを押しなさいって…

Kachou: Itsumo itte iru ja nai ka, shorui ni wa kanarazu hanko o oshinasai tte.

Section chief: I tell you all the time that you must stamp all documents with your seal.

鈴木：はい、大変申し訳ありません。

Suzuki: **Hai, taihen moushiwake ari masen.**

Suzuki: Yes. I am extremely sorry (I have no excuse).

In Japan, we believe we must apologize right away when trouble occurs with someone. It is because we care about other people and try not to upset them [see Chapter 3-2]. Especially when dealing with people important to us, such as clients or superiors, we must apologize when they make complaints. With this attitude, we demonstrate that we will give the issue consideration in deference to those people.

Of course, it is necessary to find solutions for the issues, but before anything, we attend to their feelings. However, if we do not apologize or if we make excuses, even for a small mistake, they will be annoyed. If things escalate and they become emotional, the issue can get complicated, though it could have been easily avoided.

お詫びの言葉もなかった (*owabi no kotoba mo nakatta*, there was nary a word of apology) is a set phrase when we get angry due to a lack of apology.

In some cultures, a hasty apology could be considered a detriment, so people think it is better not to apologize so readily. However, in Japan, even logical explanations can be judged as excuses, and apologizing in good faith is considered *isagiyoi* (gallant) [see Chapter 7-5].

Selected Bibliography

Benedict, R. (2006). *The Chrysanthemum and the Sword: Pattern of Japanese Culture.* Houghton Mifflin. (Original work published 1946)

Daidoji, Y. (1984). *Budoshoshinshu: The Warrior's Premier of Daidoji Yuzan.* Black Belt Communications. (Original work published circa 1725)

Doi, T. (2014). *The Anatomy of Dependence.* Kodansha International. (Original work published 1971)

Nakane, C. (1972). *Japanese Society.* University of California Press. (Original work published 1967)

Nitobe, I. (2008). *Bushido: The Soul of Japan.* Wilder Publications. (Original work published 1899)

Suzuki, D.T. (2019). *Zen and Japanese Culture.* Princeton University Press. (Original work published 1938)

Watsuji, T. (1996). *Watsuji Tetsuro's Rinrigaku: Ethics in Japan (SUNY Series in Modern Japanese Philosophy).* State University of New York Press. (Original work published 1934)

Yamamoto, T. (2014). *Hagakure: The Secret Wisdom of the Samurai.* Tuttle Publishing. (Original work published circa 1716)

Index

Conjugated verbs are shown in dictionary form.

A

aikyou 愛嬌	attractiveness	65
aiso/aisou 愛想	amiability	63–65
aiso ga ii 愛想がいい	amiable	63–64
aiso ga nai 愛想がない	not friendly	63
aiso ga tsukiru 愛想がつきる	to run out of smiles	64
aiso ga warui 愛想が悪い	unfriendly	63
aiso o tsukasu 愛想をつかす	to use up all smiles	64
aiso warai 愛想笑い	fake smile	64
aite no hara o yomu 相手の腹を読む	to read the other's mind	54
aizuchi o utsu 相づちを打つ	to pepper the conversation with responses	77
akarasama あからさま	too straight	84–85
amaeru 甘える	to rely on another's love or kindness	21–23
amayakasu 甘やかす	to spoil	21–22
anmoku no ryoukai 暗黙の了解	tacit understanding	53
atetsuke あてつけ	insinuation	88
atsukamashii あつかましい	pushy	42

B

buaisou 無愛想	not friendly	63
buenryo 無遠慮	selfish	41–42
bureikou 無礼講	informal party	68
bushidou 武士道	the way of the warrior	35, 110–113

bushi ni nigon wa nai 武士に二言はない	The warrior keeps his word once spoken.	111
bushi wa kuwane do, takayouji 武士は食わねど、高楊枝	The true warrior does not reveal his hunger.	111

C

chuu 忠	unconditional loyalty to their master	35, 113

D

deru kui wa utareru 出る杭は打たれる	The nail that sticks out gets hammered down.	51
deshabari でしゃばり	a meddler	82
deshabaru でしゃばる	to be pushy	82
desugiru 出過ぎる	to obtrude	82
do konjou ど根性	super guts	102

E

enryo 遠慮	restraint	40–44
enryo bukai 遠慮深い	with deep restraint	41–42
enryo naku 遠慮なく	without reservation	41
enryo suru 遠慮する	to decline something humbly	40, 43

G

ganbaru がんばる	to tough it out	96–98
gehin 下品	vulgar	116–117
giri 義理	sense of obligation	126–129
giri choko 義理チョコ	obligation chocolate	129
giri ga aru 義理がある	to have obligation to someone	127
giri gatai 義理堅い	having a strong sense of obligation	127
giri o kaku 義理を欠く	to be derelict in obligation to someone	128

giri to ninjou no itabasami 義理と人情の板挟み	crushed between duty and sentiment	129
goenryo kudasai ご遠慮ください	Please refrain from doing something.	42–43
guu no ne mo denai ぐうの音も出ない	utter defeat	72

H

hade 派手	flashy	121–122
haji 恥	shame	32–35
haji no bunka 恥の文化	culture of shame	34
haji o kaku 恥をかく	to disgrace oneself	32–35
haji shirazu 恥知らず	shameless	33
hara 腹	belly	54–55
hara ni mo nai koto o iu 腹にもないことを言う	to tell a white lie	54
hara no saguriai 腹の探り合い	finding each other's real intention	54
hara o kimeru 腹を決める	to make up one's mind	54
hashitanai はしたない	ill-mannered	118
hataraki bachi 働き蜂	worker bees	98
hazukashii 恥ずかしい	embarrassed	32–33
hikaeme 控えめ	restrained or moderate	80–82
hin 品	class	116–118
hin'i 品位	grace	116–117
hinkaku 品格	dignity	116–117
hinsei 品性	character	116
hitome 人目	public eye	28–31
hitome ga urusai 人目がうるさい	undue attention	29

hitome ni amaru 人目に余る	offensive	29
hitome ni tsuku 人目につく	to be noticeable	29
hitome o habakaru 人目をはばかる	to be heedful of others	29
hitome o hiku 人目をひく	to grab people's attention	29
hitome o nusumu 人目を盗む	to duck the public eye	30
hitome o sakeru 人目を避ける	to avoid the public eye	30
hitome o shinobu 人目を忍ぶ	to sneak by prying eyes	30
hitonami 人並み	average	49–51
heso magari へそ曲がり	perverse	20
honne 本音	true feelings	70–72
honne o haku 本音を吐く	to give oneself away	72
honne o morasu 本音を漏らす	to bare the truth	72
honne to tatemae 本音と建前	true feelings and official stance	70
honomekasu ほのめかす	to give a hint	84–85

I

ibushi gin いぶし銀	a matte silver finish	124
ichiban nori 一番乗り	the first to arrive	34
iji 意地	will	102
iji o haru 意地を張る	never to give in	102
iji o toosu 意地を通す	to stick to one's guns	102
ingin burei 慇懃無礼	hypocritical courtesy	68
isagiyoi いさぎよい	gallant	130–132
ishin denshin 以心伝心	good communication without speech	53, 84
issho kenmei 一所懸命	risking life to protect territory	112
isshou kenmei 一生懸命	trying one's utmost	112
iwanu ga hana 言わぬが花	some things better left unsaid	53

J

jimi 地味	plain	121–122
jouhin 上品	sophisticated	116, 123

K

kakkou ga tsukanai 格好がつかない	to look bad to people	32
kamei ni kizu ga tsuku 家名に傷がつく	honor of the family gets ruined	10
kao o dasu 顔を出す	to pop in	61
kejime けじめ	distinction	16–18
kejime o tsukeru けじめをつける	to draw a line	17
kigyou senshi 企業戦士	corporate warriors	98
kimariwarui きまり悪い	embarrassed silly	37
ki 気	life energy, spirit, mind	45–48
ki ga okenai 気が置けない	not to worry about a person because we know the situation	48
ki ni yamu 気に病む	to obsess over an issue	48
ki o kubaru 気を配る	to consider various factors	47
ki o mawasu 気を回す	to overthink the situation and dream up scenarios	48
ki o momu 気をもむ	to worry terribly about random things	47
ki o tsukau 気をつかう	to pay attention to another's needs	45–46
ki o tsukeru 気をつける	to be careful	47
kizukare (suru) 気疲れ（する）	mental fatigue	46
kokuji 国字	ideographs created in Japan	15
konjou 根性	willpower	100–102

konjou ga magatte iru 根性が曲がっている	character is twisted	101
konjou ga warui 根性が悪い	ill-natured	101
konjou o irekaeru 根性を入れ替える	to replace a bad nature with a good one	101
konjou o tataki naosu 根性をたたき直す	to reform one's character with severe training	101
konjouron 根性論	the principle of never giving up	101
koremiyogashi これみよがし	ostentatious	87–88
kouboku wa kaze ni oraru 高木は風に折らる	The towering tree will be snapped by the wind.	51
kuchi wa wazawai no moto 口は災いの元	Out of the mouth comes evil.	53
kuuki o yomu 空気を読む	to read the situation	52–53
kei wai KY	cannot read the room	52

M

menboku ga nai 面目がない	to have no honor	32
mentsu ga tsubureru 面子がつぶれる	to lose face	32
me wa kuchi hodo ni mono o iu 目は口ほどにものを言う	The eyes reveal the true meaning.	54
migurushii 見苦しい	despicable	33
mittomonai みっともない	unseemly	33–34
miuchi 身内	the inner circle	4
mizu kusai 水くさい	distant	22
mottainai もったいない	wasteful	133–136
muri 無理	unreasonable	103–105

muri ga tooreba, douri ga hikkomu 無理が通れば、道理がひっこむ	Where might is master, justice is servant.	103
muri o iu 無理を言う	to make an unreasonable request	103–104
muri suru 無理する	to do the undoable	98, 104–105
muri wa nai 無理はない	no wonder	103–104
musha shugyou 武者修行	arduous training	107

N

nadeshiko なでしこ	a Japanese pink flower	119–120
Nadeshiko Japan なでしこジャパン	The Japan National Women's Football Team	119
Nadeshiko Riigu なでしこリーグ	The Japan Women's Soccer League	119
narenareshii なれなれしい	too familiar	5
naseba naru nasaneba naranu nanigoto mo 為せば成る為さねば成らぬ何事も	Do, and it will be done; don't do, and it will never be done.	99
nemawashi 根回し	behind-the-scenes negotiation	71
ne o ageru 音をあげる	admit defeat	72
nominikeeshon 飲みニケーション	communication over drinks	61

O

oaiso お愛想	the bill at a traditional Japanese restaurant	65
okage (sama) おかげ（さま）	thanks to someone's good will	73–75
okagesama de おかげさまで	thanks to you	74
okuyukashii おくゆかしい	refined	118
on 恩	debt of gratitude	126–127
ongi ga aru 恩義がある	to be deeply indebted to a person	127
on gaeshi 恩返し	repayment for kindness	126
on shirazu 恩知らず	ungrateful	126
osato ga shireru お里が知れる	to reveal one's family background	13–14
otsukiai おつきあい	obligatory companionship	60–61

oya no kao ga mi tai 親の顔が見たい	wanting to see the parents' face	13–14
oya no kao ni doro o nuru 親の顔に泥を塗る	A child's misdeeds tarnished the honor of his parents.	10
owabi no kotoba mo nai お詫びの言葉もない	no word of apology	138

R

reigi 礼儀	manners	66–68
reigi shirazu 礼儀知らず	not knowing manners	66–67
rei ni hajimari, rei ni owaru 礼に始まり、礼に終わる	Start with a bow and end with a bow.	68

S

sabi さび	subdued refinement	123–125
sarigenai さりげない	nonchalant	85–86
seihin (ni amazuru) 清貧（に甘んずる）	honorable poverty	125, 136
seishin ittou nanigoto ka narazaran 精神一到何事か成らざらん	Where there's a will, there's a way.	99
seken 世間	society	8–11
seken ni kaomuke dekinai 世間に顔向けできない	to feel ashamed to face the world	10
seken no kaze wa tsumetai 世間の風は冷たい	Society is strict and judgmental.	9
seken shirazu 世間知らず	ignorant of the world	9
sekentei ga warui 世間体が悪い	looks bad in society	10
seppuku 切腹	suicide by cutting the belly	131
shibui 渋い	strident	122–123

shashari deru しゃしゃりでる	to poke one's nose in	83
shitashiki naka ni mo reigi ari 親しき仲にも礼儀あり	Keep good manners even among friends.	22
shitoyaka しとやか	graceful	120
shitsuke しつけ	discipline	12–15
shoujin 精進	devotion to one's research	108–109
shoujin otoshi 精進落とし	return to meat or alcohol after abstinence	108
shoujin ryouri 精進料理	the cuisine of Buddhist training	108
shoujin suru 精進する	to stay pure and focus on training	108
shugyou 修行	training	106–109
shugyou ga tarinai 修行が足りない	inadequate training	107
sotozura ga ii 外面がいい	angel outside, devil at home	6
sunao 素直	obedient and innocent	19–20
supokon スポ根	the entertainment genre of sports and guts	102

T

tatemae 建前	official stance	70–72
teki ni senaka o miseru 敵に背中を見せる	show one's back to the enemy	34
tereru 照れる	to be abashed	36–38
tere kakushi 照れ隠し	hiding one's embarrassment	38
terekusai 照れくさい	shy from praise	36
terewarai 照れ笑い	embarrassed grin	38
tereya 照れ屋	people who get easily embarrassed and shy	37
tsukiai つきあい	companionship	60–61
tsukiai ga warui つきあいが悪い	unsociable	61
tsutsumashii つつましい	modest	81–82

U

uchi うち	inside	2–7
uchi benkei 内弁慶	a lion at home, a mouse outside	6
uchi iwai 内祝い	celebration within a group	6
uchi to soto 内と外	inside and outside	2–5
uchiuchi de うちうちで	within the group	4
uchiwa no jijou o soto ni morasu 内輪の事情を外に漏らす	to leak inside information	6
ushiro kizu 後ろ傷	back cut	34

W

wa 和	peace and harmony	71
wabi わび	beauty found in poverty	123
wabi-sabi わび・さび	a taste for simplicity and for subdued refinement	123–125
wataru seken ni oni wa nashi 渡る世間に鬼はなし	Kindness can always be found in the world.	9

Y

yamato 大和	ancient Japan	119
yamato damashii 大和魂	Yamato spirit	119
yamato kotoba 大和言葉	old Japanese	119
yamato nadeshiko やまとなでしこ	the idealized Japanese woman	119–120
yoso よそ	elsewhere	2–3
yosoyososhii よそよそしい	distant in attitude	4
yosoyuki よそ行き	fancy clothes to go out	4–5

Z

zuuzuushii ずうずうしい	impudent	42

About the author

Rokuro Morita was born in Shimane Prefecture, Japan. He graduated from Waseda University in Tokyo, majoring in East Asian philosophy. After working as managing editor at Taishukan Publishing Company, he moved to Beijing, China and taught Japanese language, culture, and history at the University of International Business and Economics. Having attained the 7th-dan teacher's level in kendo, he gave classes to young people in China. He has also authored *Dual Wield in Beijing*, published by Gendai Shokan (2014), about life and teaching kendo in China. He is currently teaching at the Tokyo Central Japanese Language School.

About the supervising editor

Kiyotada Tazaki graduated from Tokyo Higher Normal School (currently Tsukuba University) and studied, as a Fulbright grantee, applied linguistics, TEFL (Teaching of English as a Foreign Language) and audiovisual education at the English Language Institute of the University of Michigan (1956–57). He authored a number of academic and professional books, such as *Anthology of English Teaching Theories and Methodology*, Taishukan Publishing Company (1995), *Dictionary of Daily American Words and Phrases*, Kodansha International (1994), *Theory of Education*, co-authored, Iwanami Shoten (1960) and many others. For consolidating the basic formula of TV language programs through his participation as a programmer and instructor in the "TV English Conversation Program" for 16 years (1961–77), he received an NHK Broadcasting and Culture Foundation Award in 1977. He is a professor emeritus of Yokohama National University and former president of Tokyo Junshin Women's College.

About the translators

Mari Williams performed in Japanese theater and television for four years, and then shifted her interest to foreign languages. After an intensive study at *Université Paris-Sorbonne*, she taught French at Oda College, Kaitani School of the Arts, and others in Tokyo. She received her M.A. in French from the University of Miami and is currently teaching Japanese and French as a senior lecturer. She is primary author of *Introduction to French Conversation*, Seitosha Publishing (1998) and has contributed numerous Japanese language articles about the cultural aspects of American life to online magazines, such as System Technology-i for English teachers in Japan. Her research focuses on Japanese language acquisition through theater, and she is currently working on an activity book using her theatrical experience.

Daniel M. Williams holds music degrees in Jazz Composition from Berklee College of Music, the University of Massachusetts, Amherst, and the University of Miami Frost School of Music. Dan studied Uechi-ryu karate in Boston and was always interested in Japanese culture, and so he accepted an offer to teach English in Japan. During his stay in Japan, he wrote and narrated articles about cross-cultural topics and life in Japan for a quarterly YMCA publication, *Pace in Terra*, and was a front-page contributor to the *Mainichi Weekly* newspaper. Dan has written music for a wide range of ensembles and taught jazz piano and music theory to all ages. He is currently completing a compendium of technical exercises for the jazz pianist. He is a black belt in JKA karate.

Decoding the Japanese Mind through Expressions

2021 年 12 月 20 日　初版　第 1 刷発行

著者　森田 六朗
翻訳　Mari Williams　Daniel M. Williams
翻訳監修　田崎 清忠

発行人　天谷 修身
発行　株式会社 アスク出版
〒 162-8558　東京都新宿区下宮比町 2-6
TEL: 03-3267-6864　FAX: 03-3267-6867
URL: https://www.ask-books.com/

装幀・DTP　アスク出版デザイン部
イラスト　yochymess
印刷・製本　株式会社 日経印刷

Original Japanese language edition published by Ask Publishing Co. Ltd.
Text copyright © Rokuro Morita

Author: Rokuro Morita
Translators: Mari and Daniel M. Williams
Supervising Editor: Kiyotada Tazaki
Designer: Ask Publishing Design Division
Illustrator: yochymess
Printing: Nikkei Printing Inc.
Publisher: ASK Publishing Co., Ltd.
2-6, Shimomiyabi-cho, Shinjuku-ku, Tokyo 162-8558 Japan
Phone: 03-3267-6864
www.ask-books.com
ISBN 978-4-86639-455-8
First edition: December 2021
Printed in Japan

All rights reserved. Reproducing all or any part of the contents is
prohibited without the permission of the publisher.